MYTHOLOGIES
of the
WORLD

MYTHOLOGIES of the WORLD
was produced for Transedition Limited
by Bender Richardson White.

Project Manager: Lionel Bender
Designer and Art Editor: Ben White
Text Editor: Michael March
Picture Research: Cathy Stastny & Lionel
   Bender

Production: Richard Johnson
Cover Design and Make-up: Mike Pilley, Radius

   Checkmark Books
   An imprint of Facts On File, Inc.
   132 West 31st Street
   New York, NY 10001

Mythologies of the world : the illustrated guide to
   mythological beliefs & customs / Michael McKenzie
   .. [et al.].
New York : Checkmark Books, 2001.
p. cm.
0–8160–4480–5 (alk. paper)
Includes bibliographical references and index.
McKenzie, Michael C.
12368859

Checkmark Books are available at special discounts
when purchased in bulk quantities for businesses,
associations, institutions or sales promotions. Please
call our Special Sales Department in New York at
(212) 967-8800 or (800) 322-8755.

You can find Facts on File on the World Wide Web at
http://www.factsonfile.com

Printed and bound in Italy

___ ___ 10 9 8 7 6 5 4 3 2 1

This book is printed on acid-free paper.

Picture Credits

The producers and publishers are grateful to the following for permission to reproduce copyright material:
t = top, b = bottom, c = center, l = left, r = right . AA = The Art Archive, COR = Corbis Images, WF = Werner Forman Archive.

Page 6: COR/Adam Woolfitt. 7: WF/Schimmel Collection. 8: COR. 9: COR/Bettmann . 10: COR/Chris Rainier. 11bl: PhotoDisc Inc. 11br: COR/Sir Edward Coly Burne-Jones /Staatsgallerie, Stuttgart . 14: COR/Roger de la Harpe. 15: COR/Archivo Iconografico. 16: COR/Jeremy Horner. 17bl: COR/Museo Capitolini/Gianni Dagli Orti. 17br: COR/Studio Patellani. 18: COR/Kevin R. Morris. 19bl: COR/Yann Arthus-Bertrand. 19br: COR/Private Collection, Peru/Nathan Benn. 20: COR/Chris Rainier. 21t: COR/Nevada Weir. 21b: COR/Michael St.Maur Sheil. 22: AA/Christie's/Eileen Tweedy. 24: COR/Musée du Louvre, Paris/Gianni Dagli Orti. 25: COR/Musée du Louvre, Paris/Gianni Dagli Orti. 26: COR/Peter Brueghel the Elder/Boymans-van Beuningen (Rotterdam, The Netherlands) Museum. 28b: AA/British Museum . 28-29: COR/Museum Deir-ez-Zor, Syria/Gianni Dagli Orti. 29cr: COR/David Lees. 30: Lionel Bender. 32: COR/Charles & Josette Lenars. 34: COR/Gianni Dagli Orti. 35tl: COR/Christine Osborne. 35br: AA. 36cr: AA /Egyptian Museum, Cairo/Gianni Dagli Orti. 36-37b: AA/British Museum/Jaqueline Hyde. 37br: COR/Gianni Dagli Orti. 38: PhotoDisc Inc./Neil Beer. 40: COR/Archivo Iconografico. 42: COR/Kevin Schafer. 44: COR/Cyprus Museum, Nicosia, Cyprus/Gianni Dagli Orti. 45t: COR/Michael Nicholson. 45b: COR/Michael Freeman. 46: COR/Ali Meyer. 47: COR/Bibliotéque des Arts de France. 48b: COR/National Archeological Museum, Naples, Italy/Araldo de Luca. 50: COR/Galleria Borghese, Rome, Italy/Gianni Dagli Orti. 52: COR/Jean Auguste Dominique Ingrés/National Gallery, London. 53: COR/Ruggero Vanni. 54: COR/Angelo Hornak. 56: COR/Francesco Solimena/National Gallery, London. 57t: COR/Gianni Dagli Orti. 57b: COR/Museo delle Terme, Rome, Italy/Gianni Dagli Orti. 58: AA/Casale Piazza Armeina, Sicily . 59t: COR/Gianni Lorenzo Bernini/Galleria Borghese, Rome, Italy. 59b: COR/House of Dionysos, Paphos/Gianni Dagli Orti. 60: COR/Filippino Lippi/Sala de Ulisse, Galleria Palatina, Florence, Italy/Arte & Immagini srl. 63: COR/Orazio Marinali/F.Zeri Collection, Mentana, Italy/Araldo de Luca. 64: A/Museo Prenesino Palestrina/Gianni Dagli Orti. 65: COR/House of Labyrinth, Pompeii/Mimmo Jodice. 66: COR/Ted Spiegel. 68: WF. 70bf: WF/British Museum, London. 70r: WF/Manx Museum, Isle of Man. 71: WF/Stofnun Arna Magnussonar a Islandi, Reykjavik, Island. 72: AA/Historiska Muséet, Stockholm/Gianni Dagli Orti. 74: WF/National Museum, Copenhagen. 75t: WF/Universitetets Oldsaksamling, Oslo, Norway. 75b: WF/Statens Historiska Museum, Stockholm. 76: COR/Enzo & Paolo Ragazzini. 78: Mary Evans Picture Library/Edouard Zier, Le Monde Illustre . 79c: Giraudon/Ivan J. Bilibin. 79b: Giraudon/Ivan J Bilibin. 80: Hutchison Library/Andrey Zvoznikov. 82: COR/Bettmann. 83bl: COR/Royal Ballet/Robbie Jack. 83br: Kim Richardson. 84: COR/Charles & Josette Lenars. 86l: WF/British Museum, London. 86r: WF/British Museum, London. 87: WF/British Museum, London. 88l: WF/Musée Royal de l'Afrique Centrale/ Turvuren. 88r: COR/The Bowers Museum of Cultural Art, California, USA.89: COR/The Purcell Team. 90: COR/Charles & Josette Lenars. 92: AA/Nakib Khan Mughal/British Library . 94: COR/National Museum of New Delhi, India/Angelo Hornak. 94-95: COR/Michael Lewis. 95: COR/National Museum of New Delhi, India/Angelo Hornak. 96t: COR/Philadelphia Museum of Art, Pennsylvania, USA. 96b: COR/Philadelphia Museum of Art, Pennsylvania, USA. 97: COR/Angkor, Siem Reap Province, Cambodia/Kevin R. Morris/Cambodia. 98: COR/Brian Vikander . 98-99: COR/Earl & Nazima Kowall. 99: COR/Lindsay Hebberd. 100: COR/Chris Lisle. 102bl: COR/Ric Ergenbright. 102br: COR/Linsay Hebberd. 103: COR/Chris Lisle. 104: COR/Ric Ergenbright. 106: AA/British Museum. 106-107: COR/Kevin R Morris. 107: Lindsay Hebberd. 108: COR/Royal Ontario Museum, Canada. 110: COR/Municipal Museum Luoyang Province, Henan Province, China/Asian Art & Archeology. 110-111: COR/Asian Art & Archeology Inc. 111: COR/Archivo Iconografico S.A. 112: COR/Lowell Georgia. 113: PhotoDisc Inc./Kim Steele. 114bl: COR/Kevin R Morris. 114br:COR/Nathan Benn. 115: COR/Galen Rowell. 116: COR/Kevin Schafer. 118bl: AA/Mireille Vautier. 118tr: WF/Schinler Collection, New York. 119: COR/Michael T Sedam. 120: COR/Buddy Mays. 121bl: COR/Tom Bean. 121tr: COR/George Lepp. 122: COR/Gary Braasch. 124cr: COR/Raymond Gehman. 124b: COR/Nathan Benn. 125:COR/Earl & Nazima Kowall. 126:PhotoDisc Inc./ Adalberto Rios. 128: WF/Museum Fur Volkerkunde, Berlin. 129t: WF/Felipe Guaman Poma de Ayala/Nick Saunders. 129b: WF/Felipe Guaman Poma de Ayala/Nick Saunders. 130t: COR/Daniel Lainé. 130b: COR/Metropolitan Museum Of Art, New York/Nathan Benn. 131: COR/Charles & Josette Lenars. 132: COR/Sergio Dorantes. 133: COR/Ric Ergenbright. 134: COR/Jeremy Horner. 135t: COR/Nevada Weir. 135b: COR/Jeremy Horner. 137: PhotoDisc Inc./Adalberto Rios. 138: PhotoDisc Inc./Adalberto Rios. 139: COR/Alison Wright. 140: COR/Charles & Josette Lenars. 142: PhotoDisc Inc./Joseph Green/Life File. 143bl: COR/Wolfgang Kaehler. 143br: COR/Penny Tweedy. 144: Veronica Strang. 145: Corbis Images. 146: Corbis Images. 147t: COR/Charles Lenars. 147b: COR/Caroline Penn. 148: PhotoDisc Inc./Adalberto Rios. 150: COR/Jack Fields. 150-151: PhotoDisc Inc. 151: COR/Roberts Holmes. 152: PhotoDisc Inc./Tim Hall.

Every effort has been made to contact copyright holders of any material reproduced in this book. Omissions or errors will be rectified in subsequent printings if notice is given in writing to Transedition Limited.

Cover photos (top row, left to right) COR/Metropolitan Museum of Art, New York/Nathan Benn; AA/Bardo Museum, Tunis/Dagli Orti; WF/Universitetets Olksasamling, Oslo. (middle row, left and right) WF/Philip Goldman Collection, London; COR/National Museum of New Dehli, India/Angelo Hornak. (bottom row, left and right) AA/Mireille Vautier; COR/Gary Braasch.

Artwork (book and cover): Reconstruction illustrations by John James. Maps by Stefan Chabluk.

The authors' acknowledgement:
Quotation on page 24 from Myths from Mesopotamia. Creation, the Flood, Gilgamesh, and others by Stephanie Dalley, page 253 (O.U.P., Oxford, 1991).

MYTHOLOGIES
of the
WORLD

The Illustrated Guide to Mythological
Beliefs & Customs

Michael McKenzie ◆ *Richard Prime*
Lisa George ◆ *Ray Dunning*

An imprint of Facts On File, Inc.

FOREWORD

When Sigmund Freud wrote confidently (barely a century ago) that religions and their attendant myths were "neurotic relics" and incompatible with modern thought, his prediction was hardly unique for the time. The prevailing winds were strongly secular, and few indeed were those who saw mythology as much more than a historical curiosity.

As we begin the 21st century, however, mythology has not only won several holding actions against its detractors, but has gone on the offensive. With the acceptance of the postmodern paradigm, and the attendant recognition that there are more "ways of knowing" than skeptical rationalism, scholars and laypeople alike are once again excited to look into mythic insights from various cultures and peoples.

I am happy to be both a contributor to, and Associate Editor of *Mythologies of the World*, and commend it highly as a readable primer on comparative mythologies. Those connected with the work have made a concerted effort to produce balanced treatments of the world's great myths, and to write both fairly and accessibly. Thus, whether you're reading about shamanism's power in Asia, Old Norse views on the afterlife, or Native American creation myths, *Mythologies of the World* presents an accurate and readable account of the world of myth.

The book's chapters correspond to different geographical regions of the world, and are arranged in the same general chronological order as the spread of mythology is regarded as having taken place. To be sure, many tribal mythologies in parts of Africa, Asia, South America and Oceania resist such neat division, but such organization nonetheless aids the reader in following the general development of mythic thought. Each chapter is divided into double-page spreads that examine, in turn, the historical development of the particular mythology, basic beliefs and the gods and goddesses, ancient rituals and customs, and present-day legacies associated with the mythology.

Extracts from well-known and important myths are interspersed throughout the book, helping to illustrate the myth's ties to both the past and the present. Each spread has a main text and various panel texts, as well as photographs and captions. Many of the panels contain extracts of specific myths, and others deal with the various traditions, customs and rituals associated with myths.

Like the other authors, I want any reference project to accomplish the goals set for it at the beginning. It was clear from the outset that this book had two primary tasks: the promotion of cultural understanding and the exploration of those deep-seated longings and drives that indelibly stamp the human race. *Mythologies of the World* meets both goals admirably, and should give the reader both enjoyment and insight into our mythic past, present and future.

Michael C. McKenzie, Associate Editor
Associate Professor of Religion, Keuka College,
Keuka Park, New York.

AUTHORS

Introduction, North America, Future of Mythology
Michael McKenzie, Ph.D., Assistant Professor of Religion and Philosophy, Keuka College, Keuka Park, New York.

Mesopotamia
Erica C.D. Hunter, Ph.D., Affiliated Lecturer in Aramaic, Faculty of Oriental Studies, University of Cambridge, England.

Egypt
Katja Goebs, Ph.D., Merton College/Oriental Institute, Oxford, England.

Greece, Rome
Lisa George, Ph.D., Assistant Professor of Classics, Arizona State University, Phoenix, Arizona.

North Europe, Central and Southern Europe
Ray Dunning, Ph.D., Mythology author and Head of Design Studies, Kingston College, England.

Africa, India, China and Japan
Richard Prime, Freelance writer and broadcaster on religion, mythology, and conservation, London, England.

Central and Southern America
Maggie Bolton, Center for Indigenous American Studies, United College, St. Andrews University, Scotland.

Oceania
Veronica Strang, Ph.D., Senior Lecturer in Anthropology, University of Wales, Lampeter, Wales.

ASSOCIATE EDITOR

Michael McKenzie is a lecturer, broadcaster, authority, and writer on comparative religious ethics, Native American religion and spirituality, and religion and postmodern culture.

Contents

INTRODUCTION

The standing stones and trilithons of Stonehenge are the most important landmarks of the grassland of Salisbury Plain in Wiltshire, England.

Primitive Tradition or Basic Need?

In the western United States, high on the dry hills overlooking the Columbia River in the State of Washington, stands a structure that stops most motorists in their tracks. It is a near full-size replica of the famous Stonehenge, the ancient stone circle on Salisbury Plain in England. And it looks strangely out of place near the farming town of Goldendale. If you explore the replica from closer up, its purpose comes starkly into focus, bringing home the power of myth.

A 6th-century B.C. carving of a fertility goddess from Anatolia.

When Samuel Hill, the famous American philanthropist, had the American Stonehenge built in the early part of the 20th century, most experts believed the original to be a series of sacrificial altars for the religious sect known as the Druids. Wishing to build a monument to the enormous sacrifice of local youth in the First World War, Hill designed the structure as a copy of the Druid monument. The fact that the Druids may not have utilized Stonehenge for that purpose, or that the original structure was built several millennia before using primitive technology, in no way detracts from the mythic power of the American structure today.

A mythic experience

When you stand among the erect and fallen stones, with the wind whistling and moaning through the massive slabs, both the meaning of Hill's work, and the power and universality of myth, become clear. The visitor *experiences* the power of myth, alive and well in the modern world. Such an understanding, however, was for a long time denigrated by many western scholars of religion, psychology, and anthropology.

The old condescension

Until fairly recently, myths and mythology were often considered to be the relics of "primitive and backward" cultures: simple stories and legends that are to be studied with detached—and perhaps bemused—"objectivity" by anthropologists and scientific researchers who knew better. It was assumed that, while the study of mythology might shed light on the beginnings of society, as the culture "matured," myths would fade from memory, like so much discarded baggage.

Changing Attitudes Toward Mythology

Western culture—especially as identified with the burgeoning disciplines of the hard sciences —was viewed as the model for all societies to emulate. There was little attention paid to stories of gods and goddesses, myths and heroes, dangerous beasts, and persistent villains. Scholars variously described mythologies as "childlike," "irrational," "primitive," and "fictional."

Religion and rationalism
Even disciplines long thought to be sympathetic to myths and mythologies, such as religion, hurried to fall into line. Religious scholars began to re-evaluate many doctrines and texts from a rationalistic or materialistic point of view, focusing on "demythologizing" the religious texts. Such ruthlessness was necessary, they said, to preserve the "true core" of traditions that arose in world views that are now viewed as "obsolete" by "modern man."

Rationalism, the notion that reason reigns supreme, and claims that all truth be subject to a materialistic sifting, were in the ascendant. But even at its height, rationalism seemed unable to come to grips with perennial questions, such as those concerning the quest for meaning. Many scholars began to recognize that even science had its limits.

Myth and postmodernism
Myths and mythologies address precisely those questions that have puzzled humanity for millennia—questions that science seems so powerless to answer. Perhaps that is why the modern academe is more open to mythic expressions of truth. In colleges and universities, postmodernity—the idea that all people speak from a particular tradition or point of view— has replaced the paradigm of modernity.

Today, the notion that there exists a "pure" reason, capable of judging myths as "obsolete" or "anti-rational," is itself outmoded. Instead, the understanding has emerged that there are many kinds of reason—a host of "rationalities"—all speaking from within their own traditions. This recent development has led to a new intellectual openness as to what myth and

An English medieval "Table of Signs" showing a man covered with figures of the zodiacal signs and a zodiac chart and calendar. In many cultures, mythology and astrology are closely linked.

mythology might mean—even as to what they might say about our humanness.

Such openness is apparent when we read the religious narratives today. We feel the power of John's gospel as he declares that "the Word has become flesh" in Jesus; we sympathize with Prince Arjuna's moral dilemma in the *Bhagavad-Gita* when he laments the terrible necessity of duty in war; we sense the truth of the importance of filial piety, whether it appears in Confucian texts, Jewish Commandments, or a Native American story; we understand when Buddha reminds us of the universality of suffering; and we are cut to the quick when different myths speak of the meaning of life and death. These narratives speak to us in ways that science never could.

The universal human experience

This change in attitude has inevitably led to a changing definition of myth. From this book's perspective, a myth is a powerful, *explanatory* narrative or story, preserved in texts or in oral traditions, that touches on the most basic human desires and needs. Some myths are explanations for the natural world, for example, how certain creatures came to be the way they are. Others run deeper, and attempt to explain the vexing and pervasive problems of humanity, including the existence or persistence of evil.

Myths, then, continue to be part of the universal human experience. They help fulfil the human desire to make sense of the world, to establish our place in the cosmos. We might suspect that, since myths seem to represent a universal human characteristic, there are modern varieties as well as ancient. And so there are. Some of them—like the myths of racial superiority—may be pernicious; others—like the 'rags-to-riches' stories common in various literary genres—may be inspiring. The latter kind illustrates precisely the modern nuance of myth that was ignored by so many previous scholars.

Myths may indeed be powerful expressions of truth. But this truth is not discovered on a petri dish, or in a theorem or postulate; it is, in the language of philosophers, "intuited" by those who experience it. Such truths lose none of their validity by being expressed in powerful stories, but gain much in terms of vividness for their audience.

Italian trader Marco Polo met Chinese emperor Kublai Khan around 1575. Polo stayed in China for 20 years then returned to Europe, bringing back stories of Chinese myths, folklore and traditions.

LOOKING AT MYTHOLOGY THEN AND NOW

Previous Assumptions	Current Views
Only "primitive" societies have myths	All societies have myths
Myths are "anti-scientific" fictions	Myths are beyond science
Myths are "anti-historical"	Myths transcend history
Mythic knowledge opposed to truth	Myths may have truths
Western society is the model for all peoples	We can learn from all societies
Logic and science dictate what is true	Truth comes in different forms
Supernatural religion is outmoded	One should be open to one's experience
Scientific method is superior	There are other ways to test truth
Myths retard "progress"	Myths may enhance humanity

Characteristics of Mythology

The modern focus on the power of myth reveals subtle differences between mythology and folklore or legends. All societies and groups have tales, stories, and legends whose origins are little known and whose purposes seem similar to those of myths and mythology. What child has not been soothed to sleep by a bedtime reading from a book of fairy tales? Who has not encountered local, regional or national tales that are part of their lore and culture? What is it that makes these stories different from myths?

Myth and folklore
Although in some instances the boundaries are blurred, there are important differences in the way myths and mythology may be viewed that distinguish them from lore and fairy tales. Significantly, myths are usually celebrated in religious traditions, especially in formal rituals that mark important aspects of the tradition.

Myths also commonly have a deep, pervasive power that acts to solidify group beliefs and values—a power that is lacking in simple folklore. Few people's lives revolve around black cats or broken mirrors, and religious rituals to celebrate them are fewer still! However, a legend can sometimes grow and mix with religious tradition, combining elements of both myth and legend. The Arthurian legend of the quest for the Holy Grail is an example of one such combination.

Myths reborn
Another characteristic of myth is its amazing resilience and flexibility of form. Because myth is so powerful, it can be reborn in another guise, for another audience, to illustrate identical or related themes to those of the original story, or even different ones. The Hebrew and Babylonian versions of the stories of the Great Flood—that epic event that signaled divine displeasure against the evils of humanity—are a case in point. Such accounts are exactly what one would expect if they had come from a common ancestor but been adapted to various cultures and religions: basic similarities, especially in the essentials, but with enough

Tribal dancers from Mount Hagen practice for a traditional ceremony in Papua New Guinea.

differences to account for the myth's travel through both space and time.

The common features in the two stories—the devious role of the snake, a plant of immortality, the divine judgment of a flood, and a boat built to escape it—suggest a common ancestry. Both stories also illustrate a loss of innocence, a forfeiture of immortality that leads inexorably to a basic human fear of death and to a deep-seated longing to live past our "three score and ten." The two stories are thus both attempts at a theodicy: an explanation of how evil and death can exist in a universe supposedly created and ruled by a beneficent god or gods. Every religion has had to make its peace with the ever-present phenomenon of death and suffering—and mythic stories provide the ideal means.

The 19th-century English artist Edward Burne-Jones's image of the Greek myth Perseus and Andromeda.

A rock painting in China of the Buddha. Buddhists believe they can end suffering by reaching nirvana—the release from the cycle of birth and death.

THE LEGEND OF THE HOLY GRAIL

Legend has it that the cup used by Jesus at the Last Supper was not lost to history but preserved in secrecy. Tales about the cup, or Grail, have divided into two related genres.

The first genre concerns Joseph of Arimathea, a rich follower of Jesus, in whose tomb Jesus was buried, and the cup's use in the Christian Church's early history. Supposedly, Joseph brought the cup from the Middle East to Britain, where it lay hidden for centuries.

The second genre built upon the first, and developed during the Middle Ages. It includes sagas about Sir Perceval (of King Arthur and the Knights of Round Table fame) and his quests to locate and possess the Grail. This variety of legend involves all the pageantry and chivalry of King Arthur's knights. The Grail is described as possessing magical properties that would benefit whichever knight was fortunate enough to find it. Such beliefs undoubtedly come from a combination of sources: early Celtic beliefs, early sayings attributed to Jesus and opinions of the time.

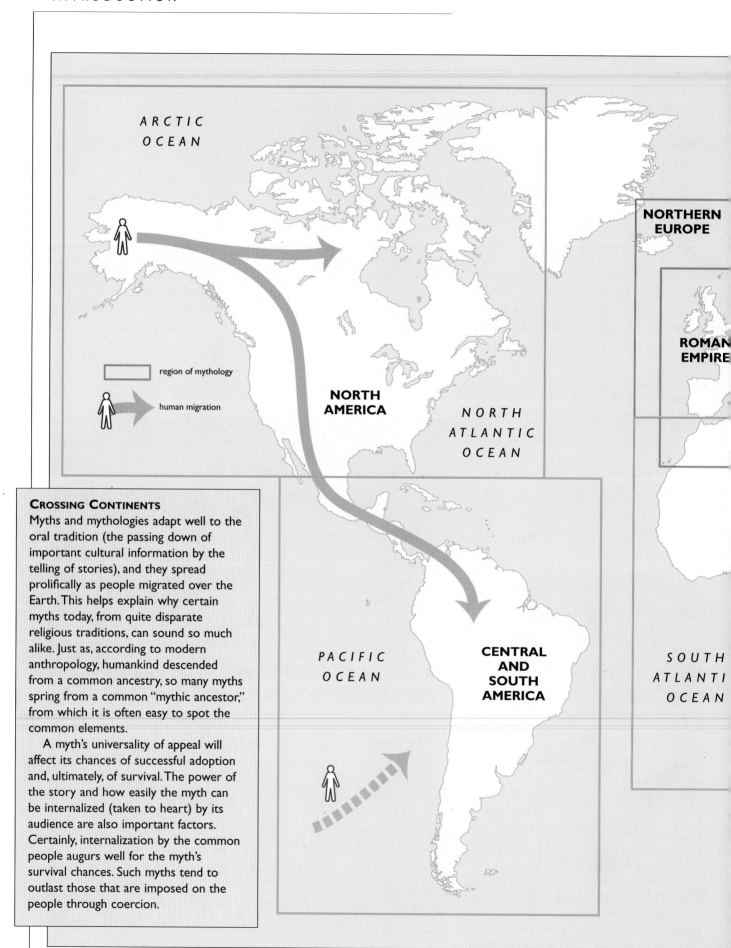

ARCTIC
OCEAN

NORTHERN
EUROPE

ROMAN
EMPIRE

region of mythology

human migration

NORTH
AMERICA

NORTH
ATLANTIC
OCEAN

PACIFIC
OCEAN

CENTRAL
AND
SOUTH
AMERICA

SOUTH
ATLANTI
OCEAN

CROSSING CONTINENTS

Myths and mythologies adapt well to the
oral tradition (the passing down of
important cultural information by the
telling of stories), and they spread
prolifically as people migrated over the
Earth. This helps explain why certain
myths today, from quite disparate
religious traditions, can sound so much
alike. Just as, according to modern
anthropology, humankind descended
from a common ancestry, so many myths
spring from a common "mythic ancestor,"
from which it is often easy to spot the
common elements.

   A myth's universality of appeal will
affect its chances of successful adoption
and, ultimately, of survival. The power of
the story and how easily the myth can
be internalized (taken to heart) by its
audience are also important factors.
Certainly, internalization by the common
people augurs well for the myth's
survival chances. Such myths tend to
outlast those that are imposed on the
people through coercion.

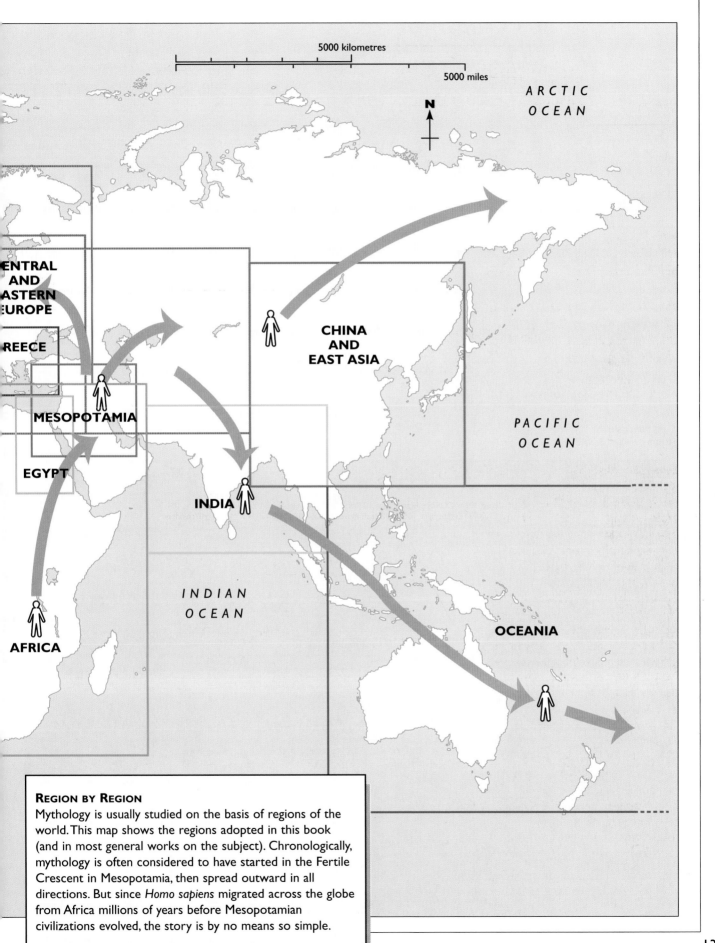

5000 kilometres

5000 miles

N

ARCTIC
OCEAN

CENTRAL
AND
EASTERN
EUROPE

REECE

MESOPOTAMIA

EGYPT

CHINA
AND
EAST ASIA

PACIFIC
OCEAN

INDIA

INDIAN
OCEAN

OCEANIA

AFRICA

REGION BY REGION
Mythology is usually studied on the basis of regions of the
world. This map shows the regions adopted in this book
(and in most general works on the subject). Chronologically,
mythology is often considered to have started in the Fertile
Crescent in Mesopotamia, then spread outward in all
directions. But since *Homo sapiens* migrated across the globe
from Africa millions of years before Mesopotamian
civilizations evolved, the story is by no means so simple.

The Quest for Meaning

Humanity's ancient quest for meaning has left its traces. All over the world, from the Australian outback and islands of the Pacific to the plains and mountains of Europe, Africa, and Asia, prehistoric people left drawings, paintings, sculptures, and etchings, most of them with uncertain meaning, but some with obvious mythic overtones.

Pictographs (drawings or paintings on rocks) and petroglyphs (etchings in rock) usually depict everyday hunting or fishing scenes. In some instances, they clearly represent totemic images—animals chosen by a clan or tribe for their physical or mental traits, such as the hunting prowess of an eagle. In other cases, the rock images may relate to a local shaman, the spiritual leader of a local tribe who derives his power from a specific animal.

Rock sculptures

There is a similar diversity of meaning within rock sculptures. Many stone figurines have been found in the Middle East and elsewhere with exaggerated female characteristics. They probably represent a connection between female fertility and the desired fecundity of the land. In many of the ancient agricultural regions, the Earth was commonly associated with the goddess of fertility, and the rain with the male god who fertilized the ground—much like the male semen fertilizing the female egg.

In other instances of rock art, such as the gigantic statues of Easter Island, there is no certain explanation for their

Painting of eland, gazelle and hunters from the Kamberg rock shelter in the Drakensberg Mountains of eastern South Africa. Eland, giraffe and elephants were popular subjects of the hunter-gatherer San, or Bushmen, artists of the Kalahari Desert.

"The Great Black Cow" cave painting at Lascaux, France. The pictographs here are believed to have been created between 15,000 and 30,000 years ago.

existence. The myths that explained them have passed away with their authors, and all we are left with as to their purpose is conjecture.

Explaining the universe

One of the greatest and most persistent themes in mythology is cosmogony—an explanation for the creation and maintenance of the universe. Since history began, people have pondered their existence and their place in the cosmos.

In the Babylonian Creation Myth, the universal themes of struggle, usurpation and familial conflict emerge to attach to a world that is—literally–born from strife and violence. Such themes are common to various cosmogonical myths, and relate well to the all-too-familiar human experience of conflict, struggle, and death.

ENUMA ELISH (BABYLONIAN CREATION MYTH)

In the beginning, there are two deities, Apsu and Tiamat, the freshwater and saltwater gods. Their union produces a plethora of deities, most notably Ea, the god of magic and wisdom.

Apsu desires to destroy this new generation of gods, but Ea acts first and destroys Apsu, before producing yet another deity, Marduk. The widowed Tiamat plots revenge on Ea, enlisting the help of Ea's half-brother, Kingu. Marduk, like his father Ea, does not lack ambition, and decides to defend Ea for his own ends.

In a cosmic battle, Marduk slays Tiama, and binds Kingu to an eternal prison. Marduk and Ea then cleave Tiamat's body in two, forming heaven and Earth. Now, Marduk reigns supreme in both power and wisdom.

Prehistoric people used a variety of natural pigments to create rock paintings. Colors were mostly red, black, yellow, and brown. In caves, they worked by the light from animal-fat lamps. The sites were probably used for rituals before hunts or as places of worship to spirits.

Myth and Virtue

Almost all mythic accounts emphasize certain values and virtues thought to be essential to people. The *Rig-Vedas*, one of the most important scriptures of Hinduism, underscores the necessity of sacrifice to appease the gods. It also gives divine sanction for the social caste system and the idea of priests as intermediaries between gods and humans. Similarly, accounts from the Native Americans of North America exemplify certain values and the maintenance of a way of life that is respectful not only to the "Great Spirit" above, but to the traditional ways of the elders.

Significantly, the Native American Yakama people's creation myth supports various religious beliefs such as ani-mism—the idea that absolutely everything in the universe may be alive. The audience of such a story would not only think that the mountains described were "alive" in a very real sense, but that it was perfectly normal to hear the voices of ancestors coming from them.

Divine intervention

Divine sanction is a potent force behind myth. Gods and goddesses are active, and their demands upon the people often constitute the myth's lesson. For example, in the Hindu scripture the *Bhagavad-Gita*, Prince Arjuna's reluctance to wage war against his friends and relatives is only overcome when Krishna, a manifestation of the deity Vishnu, intervenes.

Arjuna must fight, Krishna points out, because it is his *dharma*, his duty as a warrior to do so. In this way, the caste system is also divinely reinforced. Krishna reminds Arjuna that any killing that takes place is merely the killing of the body. The spirit (or *atman*) is inviolate and cannot be destroyed; it will reappear in another incarnation. Moreover, says Krishna, Arjuna's opponents—like all humans—are designed for death, and the Prince cannot change their fate. Thus, the *Bhagavad-Gita* reinforces important elements of the Hindu religion, and the myth achieves much of its power through an authoritative role for Krishna.

The gods of Greek myths

Gods and goddesses also play major roles in shaping human affairs in Greek myths. The ancient Greeks viewed the writings of Homer in much the same way as western culture views the Bible. The mythic tales of adventure, war and valour are paradigmatic for illustrating the moral life.

In Homer's *Illiad*, which portrays the war between the Greeks and Trojans, victory for the Greeks is assured—but just barely—because most of the strongest gods supported them. In Homer's other great epic, the *Odyssey*, divine action alone

At Huilloc in the highlands of Peru, locals conduct a Pachamama (Mother Earth) offering of plants.

insures the survival of the hero of the story, Odysseus. The message behind these stories was clear to the Greek audience. To achieve success in life, not only must you not offend the gods, but you must also appease the more powerful ones, such as Zeus and his allies, through proper behavior and ritualistic sacrifice.

The links between the mythic tales of Homer, the Greek gods and Greek virtues—justice, wisdom, courage, and balance—were acknowledged throughout Greek society. Greek mythology greatly influenced the conquering Romans, and left an indelible mark on western society that lasts to the present day.

A Greek vase from around 550 B.C. showing a scene from the myth of Theseus and the Minotaur.

THE YAKAMA CREATION MYTH

In the beginning of the world, everything was water, and the Great Chief Above lived by himself. Deciding to make the world, he created it out of mud, which hardened into dry land and rocks. He made all that there is on Earth, the trees, roots, and berries, out of mud, and then finally he made man. He told the man to take game from the woods, berries from the land, and fish from the waters.

When the man became lonely, the Great Chief Above made a woman to be his companion, and went on to teach the woman to dress in skins, find roots and berries and make baskets. She and the man lived together and enjoyed all that the Great Chief Above had given them.

Despite all that they had, the couple began to quarrel, and the Mother Earth became angry. She shook the land so hard that mountains fell down, damming the streams and making waterfalls and lakes. Many people were killed by the violent shaking.

Someday, the Great Chief Above will overturn the fallen mountains, and the spirits of those killed by the landslides will go back into their bodies. Right now, their spirits live in the tops of the mountains and watch over the people below. One can hear their voices still, and the people below know that their ancestors are always near. No one knows when the Great Chief Above will do this, but the spirits of those who have died will only return to those who kept the beliefs of their grandfathers.

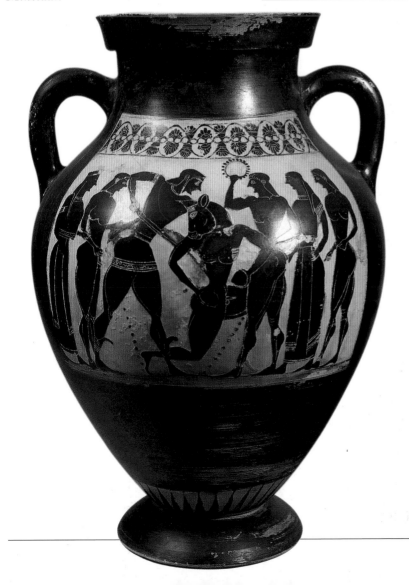

A painted tribesman of Zaire performs a traditional dance that preserves his people's elaborate mythology. In many ancient African cultures, masked dancing provides a link between the spiritual world and society at large.

Spirit and Visions

Faces and bird figures carved on a wooden totem pole in British Columbia, Canada. Totem animals include cougars, ravens, salmon, and eagles, which possess traits highly prized by humans and are associated with the gods.

M yths assisted humans not only in reaching up to the gods, but in searching for ethics that would apply to both people and nature. Whereas many mythic stories demonstrated how divine power influenced humans, and should be heeded at all costs, others spelled out the animistic beliefs held by those societies.

The spirit quest

Animistic rituals, which were part of Native American mythology, included the spirit (or vision) quest. This was a rite associated with puberty, and usually with the male members of the tribe. The young boy would be sent out alone on a mission to find his "spirit power," which would guide him for the rest of his life.

The quest could last for weeks and often meant staying in a remote and desolate location, without food and with little water. The spirit power would come from the animal that would give the youth a particular power associated with that animal, such as keen eyesight from the hawk. Ever after, tribal members would associate him with that animal. After a formal naming ceremony, the man—now no longer a boy—would begin to take his rightful place in the tribe.

After his spirit quest, the young Wakwei grew up to be the famous Smohalla ("Dreamer"), who founded the Native American revivalist religion Washani. Smohalla always claimed to have received

the religion—which advocated a total return to traditional ways–during his vision quest on La Lac mountain.

Totemism

Another concept common in the study of religion and myth and associated with spirits and animals is totemism. "Totem poles"—large, wooden sculptures of various animals, usually carved out of whole cedar trees—are a familiar example.

In totemism animals range from quasi-divine creatures to intermediaries between the deities and human beings. They are accessible to the families, tribes, or clans that venerate the creatures, and are capable of sharing with them their power and wisdom. The animals are usually—but not always—represented in a physical form, such as a totem pole, for the purposes of ritual and ceremony.

Two thousand years ago, the Nazca of southern Peru made huge images of plants and animals in the stony desert. The images may have been symbols to the sky gods.

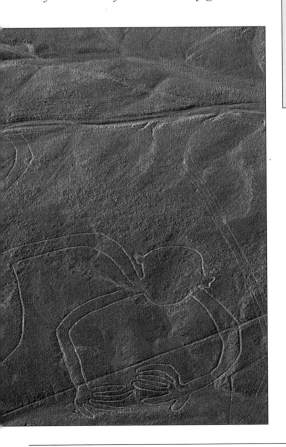

SMOHALLA'S VISION QUEST

From his earliest memory, Wak-wei knew he was different. Born along the great river (now called the Columbia), his parents had seen the first white men to appear in that country. They called themselves "Lewis" and "Clark."

Wak-wei was never proud of his body—his short legs, large head, and hunched back made him the object of many childhood jokes. His parents, however, told him that the Great Spirit had a reason for making him that way, and that he was a special creation. Wak-wei never forgot what his parents had told him, and he always paid close attention to what all the elders said. Soon, all the leaders of the boy's tribe recognized Wak-wei's native intelligence—after all, the boy had come from a long line of shamans and native prophets. They told him, "Wak-wei, you must go and find your spirit power. Perhaps you can help us, and tell us what to do about the many white people who are here."

So, one spring day, when the Sun was warm along the river, and the rabbit brush was full of yellow flowers, Wak-wei decided to begin his quest. He had decided to go to La-Lac, a high desert mountain about one day's travel from his

village. After bidding his parents farewell, he began the steep climb up the mountain.

On reaching the top, Wak-wei realized that, although it was warm along the river, it felt like winter up on the mountain. Drifts of snow were everywhere, and the wind howled like speel-yi, the coyote. After piling up some rocks for shelter, and lining it with small brush, Wak-wei sat down to wait. He spent many days nearly freezing to death, with only some bits of dried salmon for food. Then he heard the voice of the crow calling to him, telling him to lead his people. And he also heard the voice of speel-yi. Like the crow, it spoke to Wak-wei: "Lead your people back to the ways of the grandfathers."

Wak-wei knew he had been given a great gift, to hear the voices of two animals, to receive both of their spirit powers. As he made his way back down the mountain, Wak-wei knew he would always remember that day.

Conquistadores found many examples of elaborate metalworking among Andean people, usually of animals, gods, and supernatural creatures.

Religion and Myth

Religion and myth both deal with the deepest-seated human elements and emotions. In comparing them and exploring relationships between them, a number of common themes emerge. First, myths, like religion, tend to be celebrated or commemorated by what is known as "ritual." Rituals are planned actions or ceremonies that occur in formalized settings.

Hindu marriage
Marriage is one of the most common rituals in which both religion and myth play a part. It is celebrated by all religions, yet different traditions implant and institutionalize their myths into the ceremony in different ways. For instance, the Hindu ceremony of marriage is a rich tapestry of myth and ritual, designed to unite the bride and groom in a union blessed with fertility. Both bride and groom make offerings of rice during the ceremony,

before the focus shifts to the woman, as she pours more rice into a sacred fire. In some Hindu ceremonies, the bride then steps on a millstone used to grind rice, and with her partner walks on other piles of rice. The central place given to rice suggests the mythic importance of fertility, and the hope that the couple's union will be blessed with children.

Priestcraft and localized gods
The second common theme that joins religion and myth is what is called priestcraft. Many religions were started by a charismatic leader or founder, such as Buddha, Jesus, or Moses. After the leader's death, the religion undergoes a crisis. Often a struggle ensues over how to interpret the many myths and stories surrounding the founding of the tradition. Nearly always, a class of people emerges, called priests, who claim to possess the divine authority to interpret the sacred myths of the tradition. The priests usually become established, as few would dare to challenge such authority and power.

The third theme, which relates to the second, concerns the place of sacrifice in solidifying the mythic structure of the religion. Many religious traditions required the death of animals—and sometimes humans—to appease the gods, and to underscore the importance of complying with any covenants between humans and deities.

Yet another common theme is the mythic understanding that the deities are associated with a particular place—whether a city, a village, or a region. When that place flourishes, the god or gods are said to be happy. When it is invaded or pillaged, this demonstrates the gods'

The Dani of Indonesia every few years celebrate "Mauwe," a festival in which boys are initiated to manhood, marriages are arranged, old quarrels are settled, and the spirits are appeased with offerings of pigs.

abandonment of the people. It was not until the beginnings of the Hebrew religion in the Middle East that a god was envisioned who ruled the whole world.

Why study myths?

Myths provide us with more than merely fodder for historical curiosity. Indeed they can teach us something about ourselves. The fact that myths have not gone away, that they are pervasive and powerful components of the human experience, suggests that human beings, in the words of Aristotle, will forever "seek to know."

Moreover, myths show that the spiritual quest is neither empty nor lonely. Most religious myths strive to enhance the community and to strengthen links between members of the human family. Whether one studies the stories of the Bushmen of Africa, the hieroglyphic texts of the ancient Pharaohs, or the mythic wisdom of ancient China or Japan, it is frankly exhilarating to hear their voices resonate and to understand human community in this way.

But mythology can also teach us about our own world and our responsibilities towards it. In the mythic voices from the Australian outback, an Egyptian temple, or a Native American tale, we encounter the respect for the environment that many narrative myths teach so well. Allied to that respect, myths suggest, are a human frailty and a tendency toward what the Greeks called hubris, or unseemly pride. Perhaps the most fitting illustration of how myths can both inspire and warn comes—appropriately enough—in a myth.

In Greek mythology, Daedalus and his son Icarus are imprisoned in the tortuous maze known as the Labyrinth. To escape, Daedalus crafts two sets of wings—one for himself and one for his son. But successful escape turns into tragedy as Icarus, who is enthralled by his power to soar ever higher toward the Sun, flies too high, allowing the Sun's

heat to melt the wax that holds his wings. The lesson of Icarus, and of myths in general, may be that it is noble to aspire to great heights, but humans should always keep at least one foot firmly planted in reality. Such morals are indeed timeless, and ensure that myths will remain a part of the human experience.

An offering is held up at the celebration of the Inti Raimi festival in Peru. It is the priests who often take on the task of administering offerings and sacrifices.

A masked tribal dancer at Victoria, Zimbabwe. In many African ceremonies, masks could be worn only by those men who had gone through an initiation process involving religious rituals and customs.

CHAPTER 1

MESOPOTAMIA

Terracotta plaque of Ishtar, the Mesopotamian goddess of love and war. She is winged, has bird's talons, and stands nude, except for the horned crown, which was the symbol of the gods.

The Gods and Their Cities

CANAANITE MYTHOLOGY
Canaanite mythology was strongly influenced by Mesopotamia, but developed its own distinct regional flavor. Canaanite myths and religious practices are often referred to in the Bible, but in a negative way. Rich hoards of Canaanite texts were found at Ras Shamra (Ugarit), on the Mediterranean coast of Syria, during excavations in 1929. Discoveries at the ancient city of Mari, on the River Euphrates in eastern Syria, included prophetic texts, in which messages from the gods were conveyed through ordinary people.

The origins of the myths of Mesopotamia belong to a time when writing had not yet been invented. Stories of local gods and heroes were told and retold many times over before they began to be written down some 5,000 years ago, after the emergence of the first cities.

Sumer and Akkad

Around 4000 B.C., people began to live in cities that grew up on the fertile plain of Sumer. These cities boasted great temple complexes, which in power, wealth and influence compared to monasteries in medieval Europe. The Sumerians believed that the temples were the estates of the gods and goddesses, whom they treated like humans. The priests and priestesses who served in the temples even fed and clothed their deities.

The kingdom of Akkad came to dominate the region in about 2300 B.C. under Sargon, who, according to legend, had been found as a baby in a basket among bulrushes. The Akkadians assimilated much of the Sumerian culture, including the mythology, but gave some of the gods new names. For example, Enki, the Sumerian god of fresh water, became Ea.

Role of the gods

Each of the Mesopotamian cities had a patron god or goddess to keep the city prosperous and protect it in times of war. Anu, the father of the gods, was the patron god of Uruk, while the god of Babylon was Marduk. Enlil, the storm god, was the patron of Nippur, where he lived with his wife, the goddess Ninil, and son, Ninurta.

Gods and goddesses also had national responsibilities. They chose the king that would preside over all the Mesopotamian city-states. This was done periodically, as the office of king was not hereditary but rotated among the different city-states. The deities cast their votes at a divine council, which always met at the city of Nippur, and they took an oath to abide by the council's decision.

The first civilizations—and first written mythologies—are considered to have evolved in Mesopotamia, which was bounded on the west by the River Euphrates and on the east by the River Tigris. This region of arable land was first settled in the south by the Sumerians. They were conquered by the Akkadians, a Semitic people who made Babylon their power center and Babylonia their kingdom. Later still, the Assyrians dominated the region.

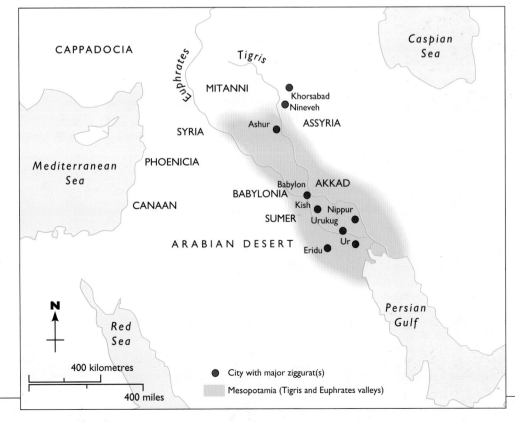

CAPPADOCIA

MITANNI

Tigris

Euphrates

Caspian Sea

Khorsabad
Nineveh

SYRIA

Ashur   ASSYRIA

Mediterranean Sea

PHOENICIA

CANAAN

Babylon   AKKAD
BABYLONIA
Kish
SUMER   Nippur
Urukug

ARABIAN DESERT
Ur
Eridu

Persian Gulf

N

Red Sea

400 kilometres

400 miles

● City with major ziggurat(s)

Mesopotamia (Tigris and Euphrates valleys)

Forces of Nature

King Hammurabi praying before Shamash, who wears the divine horned crown and holds in his right hand his symbol, the Sun's ray. Wings sprout from his shoulders. This stele dates from about 1780 B.C.

THE BABYLONIAN STORY OF CREATION
When the goddess Tiamat, who personified the sea, and a host of demons, threatened the gods, Marduk offered to kill her, on the condition that, if successful, he would become supreme god. After some terrifying battles, he shot an arrow that pierced her belly, split her down the middle, and slit her heart, vanquished her and extinguished her life. He threw down her corpse and stood on top of her.

From her body, Marduk created the Milky Way. The rivers Tigris and Euphrates flowed from her eyes. The other gods were very relieved, and bestowed kingship on Marduk. In return, he fashioned a "primeval" human to do the work of the gods so that they could live lives of leisure.

MESOPOTAMIAN GODS, GENIES, AND DEMONS

An *apkallu*, or sage

Each kingdom and city tended to have not only its own group of gods and goddesses, but also its own demons, spirits, and ghosts.

The gods and goddesses of Mesopotamia represented the forces of nature upon which the prosperity of Sumer and Akkad depended. The head of the pantheon was Anu, the sky god, whose name means "heaven." His son was Enlil, god of winds and storms. Enlil himself later became king of the gods, before he, in turn, was replaced by Marduk, who defeated the forces of Chaos. Enki, Enlil's son, was the god of fresh or "sweet" water and the source of all magical, secret power. He lived at Eridu and instructed humans in the arts and crafts.

The Sun and Moon gods
Next in importance, after the sky, winds, and freshwater gods, were the Sun and Moon gods. Utu, the Sumerian Sun god was the enemy of darkness and evil, dispelling disease with "the healing that was in his wings." He was also the god of justice. His name later changed to Shamash,

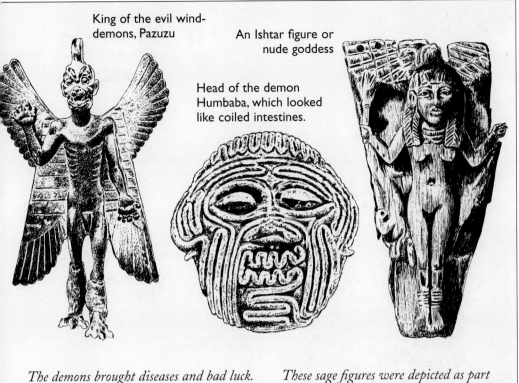

King of the evil wind-
demons, Pazuzu

An Ishtar figure or
nude goddess

Head of the demon
Humbaba, which looked
like coiled intestines.

*The demons brought diseases and bad luck.
The royal palaces at Nimrud were decorated
with painted stone reliefs of* apkallu.

*These sage figures were depicted as part
human, part animal. The* apkallu *protected
kings and also dispensed fertility.*

THE EPIC OF GILGAMESH

Gilgamesh, a king of the Sumerian city of Uruk in the 3rd millennium B.C., is remembered as the semi-divine hero of *The Epic of Gilgamesh*, which was very popular in Mesopotamia and throughout the Near East.

With his best friend, the wild man Enkidu, Gilgamesh set off on a series of adventures. Together they defeated the monster Humbaba, then killed the Bull of Heaven after Gilgamesh spurned the goddess Ishtar's offer of marriage. When Enkidu died, Gilgamesh went on a quest for eternal life. After safely crossing the Waters of Death, he met the immortal man, Ut-napishtim, who told Gilgamesh how he and his family had survived a great flood.

The Plant of Eternal Youth, Ut-napishtim said, grew at the bottom of the sea. Gilgamesh found it, but while he was bathing one evening, a snake ate the precious plant and he had to return empty-handed to Uruk. Gilgamesh's search for immortality had come to nothing.

the Akkadian word for "Sun." In Sumerian times, the Moon god was called Nanna and was worshiped at the city of Ur. Later, Nanna took the Akkadian name Sin. His symbol was a crescent moon.

Sin had a daughter, Ishtar (Sumerian "Inanna"), who became associated with the planet Venus. She was the goddess of love and sex—notorious for being insatiable and fickle. The most important of her many lovers was Dumuzi (later called Tammuz, a god of fertility and vegetation.)

MYTH OF HOW THE SEASONS BEGAN

The goddess Ishtar descended to the Underworld. She passed through seven gates and at each one was stripped of a piece of her clothing. When she reached her sister, the goddess Ereshkigal who was queen of the Underworld, Ishtar was naked. She fell ill and all fertility on Earth ceased. Ea, the god of water, wisdom, and magic, tried to rescue her, but failed. However, Ereshkigal spared Ishtar, who returned to the Earth to find all her servants in mourning but her lover Dumuzi enjoying himself. So she banished him to the Underworld for part of each year ever after.

DEITIES AND MYTHS OF CANAAN

Many Mesopotamian gods were also known in Canaan but under different names. Ishtar was famous as Astarte all over the Middle East. El, a Semitic word that meant "god," was the chief god of the Canaanites and father of the divine family, like the Mesopotamian god Anu. El also sanctioned decisions that were made at a heavenly court presided over by his son Baal.

Mesopotamian myths traveled with the gods to Canaan. Like Marduk, Baal, the god of storms, thunder, and rain, fought the Sea, defeating her with the help of magical clubs. This conflict may be what is alluded to in the Old Testament of the Bible:

*With his stong arm he cleft the sea-monster and struck down the Rahab [the Sea] by his skill.
By his breath the skies are clear
and his hand breaks the primeval sea-serpent.*
(Job 26:12–13)

*Cylinder seals, like this one from the late 3rd millennium B.C.,
often bore mythological subjects. Gilgamesh was especially popular.*

Mighty Landmarks

THE TOWER OF BABEL
The ziggurat at Babylon gave rise to the story of the Tower of Babel in the Old Testament (Genesis 11:1–9), where Babylon is portrayed as a decadent city, in contrast to the uprightness and purity of Jerusalem. This theme continues in the New Testament, which describes Babylon as "the mother of all harlots and abominations of the Earth" (Revelation 17:5). Even today, in Western thinking the name "Babylon" conjures up images of decadence and depravity. The ziggurat at Babylon was called Etemenanki, meaning "the temple of the foundation of heaven and Earth." The whole edifice was demolished by the Assyrian king Sennacherib in 689 B.C., when his forces defeated the Babylonians.

The Tower of Babel captured the imagination of such European painters as Pieter Brueghel the Elder.

Mesopotamian temples were places of worship, ceremony, and economic centers where much of the city's wealth was concentrated. Like cathedrals in medieval Europe, the temples were prominent features of the city. At Uruk two magnificent temples occupied more than one-third of the city. One was for the sky god Anu, the other for his daughter Inanna (Ishtar).

Temples were designed and built on a "tripartite" plan, consisting of a long central chamber and side rooms, with a stepped altar at one end. The statue of the god to whom people made offerings stood on the altar, which faced the temple entrance. Staircases led to the roof, where sometimes the priests said prayers. Some priests in the temple specialized in divination and exorcism. The temples also supported many craftsmen and artisans. Canaanite temples followed the Mesopotamian tripartite design, which influenced the building of the temple in Jerusalem by King Solomon.

ZIGGURATS
Ziggurats were huge, mud-brick structures. They consisted of a series of superimposed platforms topped by a temple. Temples on platforms were built at Eridu as early as 5000 B.C., but the first real ziggurats did not appear till 2000 B.C.

Ziggurats were similar in shape to the stepped pyramids of Egypt, but unlike pyramids, ziggurats were not tombs. The design symbolized a sacred mountain and represented the human desire to be close to the gods. This illustration shows the ziggurat at Ur, with the temple of the Moon god Nanna on the top.

BUILT OF MUD BRICKS
Ziggurats were constructed of Sun-dried mud bricks. Some had an outer covering of baked brick.

PRIESTS
Many orders of priests spent their lives in the temple, serving the goddess and attending to her every need. Priests also administered Nanna's estate, ensuring that the temple received agricultural produce from the region.

THE GREAT FLOOD STORY

Stories of a Great Flood that were preserved in Mesopotamian myths passed into the Old Testament (Genesis 7–9). Many of the similarities are striking.

Like Noah in the Bible, in *The Epic of Gilgamesh* the immortal man Ut-napishtim built a great boat and loaded it with gold, silver, and all the beasts as well as his family. He also sent out a dove, a swallow and a raven to search for dry land after the terrible storms and floods, in the same way as Noah sent out the dove three times.

Yet, there are also fundamental differences, highlighting major changes in the divine role. *The Epic of Gilgamesh* describes the gods as "like flies gathered over the sacrifice" that Ut-napishtim had prepared as a thanksgiving. By contrast, the Old Testament portrays the majesty of a supreme God who establishes a covenant with Noah, saying,

My (rain)bow I set in the cloud
sign of the covenant
between myself and Earth.
(Genesis 9:13).

OFFERINGS TO THE GODS
Citizens brought gifts for Nanna, placing them on stone offering tables. They also donated small statues of people praying. These were placed next to emblems of Nanna to worship continuously for the life of the donor. Animal sacrifices were carried out in many temples.

AT THE ALTAR
Rulers and important citizens regularly performed ceremonies at the altar to Nanna in order to ward off evil and achieve longevity. Only the High Priest could enter the Holy of Holies, or the sacred innermost chamber of the temple, which was the abode of Nanna.

GARDENS
Trees were planted around the walls to beautify the ziggurat, just as Babylon was believed to have the "Hanging Gardens," one of the Seven Wonders of the Ancient World. Enlil's temple, which stood on top of the ziggurat at Nippur, was called the "mountain house." It was the holiest shrine in Mesopotamia, since kingship was thought to have descended from the heavens at this point.

THE WHITE TEMPLE OF URUK
The first great temples emerged with the rise of cities in Sumer. The "White Temple" at Uruk was built in about 4000 B.C. It stood on a high terrace that enclosed the remains of two earlier buildings. The central chamber featured a colonnade 30 meters wide with columns 2 meters in diameter supporting a roofed hall. The columns were decorated with thousands of clay cones, painted red, black, and white and arranged in striking patterns.

This complex was levelled and rebuilt several times, each time raising the temple platform. Eventually these structures turned into ziggurats.

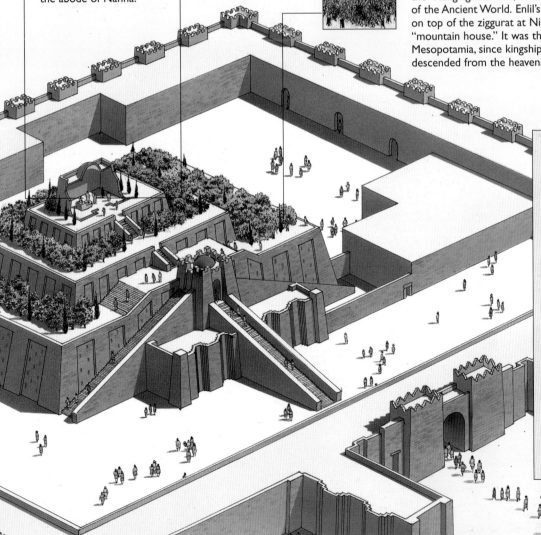

Festivals, Ceremonies, and Prayers

Throughout the year, many festivals for the gods were held in the great temples of Mesopotamia. These celebrations were state occasions and they lasted for many days. To make the land fertile and the cities prosper, it was vital for such ceremonies to take place every year.

Marriage and regeneration

Sumerian texts refer to the ancient Sacred Marriage Rite, which was first performed more than 5,000 years ago at Uruk. Scenes from this ceremony are also carved on an alabaster vase that dates to around 3000 B.C. Each year, the king of Uruk, representing the god Dumuzi, would bring the harvest of dates as a wedding gift to the temple of Inanna (later called Ishtar), who was his bride. The high priestess, representing the goddess, opened the storehouse for the king. After he entered the temple, the couple would enact a ritual of sexual intercourse to ensure that the future harvests would be abundant.

The myth of Ishtar's descent to the underworld ended with instructions for an annual ritual to commemorate Tammuz (Dumuzi), the god of fertility and vegetation. Every year, a Death Drama was performed in the sweltering summer months of Tammuz (June and July). A statue of the dead god that had been washed and anointed lay in state while large bands of mourners lamented his death. Tammuz's resurrection and return to Ishtar symbolize an agricultural cycle of seasonal death and regeneration that is echoed in the Greek myth of Persephone and her mother Demeter.

New year celebrations

The ten-day annual Akitu festival at Babylon was held in the month of Nisan (April). An ancient cuneiform tablet gives detailed instructions on how this festival to ensure cosmic order for the New Year was celebrated.

After four days, the *Enuma Elish* (Babylonian Creation Myth) was recited, accompanied by a dramatic reenactment of the epic battle between Marduk and

THE WARKA VASE
The Warka vase was originally one of a pair. It is more than 1 meter tall and was found in a temple treasure hoard at Uruk. The top band shows the procession of the king bringing the produce to the temple of the goddess. A female figure who is identified by reed standards that were the symbol of Inanna receives a basket of dates, which is carried by a naked man. The lower bands on the vase show plants and animals, as well as naked servants, possibly priests, who carry containers with produce.

The Warka vase, dating from around 3000 B.C.

This model of a liver, made from clay, was used in divination rituals. It is divided into separate sections and annotated to help the diviner make interpretations.

Tiamat. Marduk was then returned to his temple, which was sprinkled with water and fumigated with incense. A sheep was sacrificed to remove all the city's sins, and in the presence of his court the king ceremonially abdicated his office, kneeling humbly before the statute of the god and vowing to uphold justice and honor. He was then reinstated as king. On the tenth day, a "banquet of the gods" celebrated the passing of the crisis and the "fixing of destinies" for the coming year.

Private worship

As well as participating in the great festivals to ensure the good fortune of their city and state, Mesopotamian people sought the help of gods and goddesses in their private lives. People placed statues in temples to act on their behalf and pray for them. Success in personal life was thought to be due to the personal interest that a deity took in a man and his family. Misfortune, on the other hand, was believed to be due to demonic possession.

READING THE FUTURE

To ascertain what the gods and goddesses expected of them, people of Mesopotamia consulted priests who specialized in interpreting the future. The priests used a variety of techniques, including divination, reciting incantations, and writing inscriptions on amulets.

One of the most popular forms of divination was extipiscy. A sheep or goat would be sacrificed, and its heart, lungs, or liver were interpreted by observing their form and shape, rather like palmists reading the palms of their clients today.

Mesopotamian practices were borrowed by the Canaanites. A set of three-dimensional models of sheep livers was found during excavations at the palace at Mari. Two versions of a long incantation against the bite of a venomous snake were also discovered at Ugarit. Throughout the Middle East, amulets in the form of terracotta or metal models of the goddess Astarte, naked and displaying her sexual organs, were very popular.

Statues with hands clasped in reverential prayer, that were placed in temples, to pray for the well-being of their donors. The eyes were inlaid with shell, lapis lazuli, and bitumen.

CANAANITE FESTIVALS
Marduk's victory in the Babylonian Creation Myth is paralleled in Baal's defeat of the god of death and in the Israelite concept of the Kingship of God. The mythological imagery of the Baal myths and the Canaanite New Year liturgy occur in some of the Psalms of the Old Testament.
The Lord is king; he is clothed in majesty; the Lord clothes himself with might and fastens on his belt of wrath ...The Lord on high is mightier far than the noise of great waters, mightier than the breakers of the sea.
(Psalm 93:1)

CHARMS FOR ALL OCCASIONS
Amulets were used for many purposes. Some were for good fortune in travel or success in love. Others were hung up in houses to protect their occupants from disease. When someone fell ill, the demon causing the illness had to be persuaded to leave the body of the sick person. Some amulets were inscribed with texts from myths; others depicted the demons.

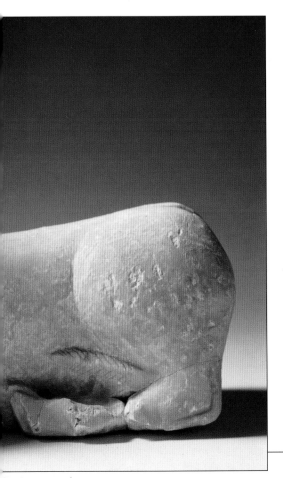

Human-headed, winged bull-figure from Nebi Yunus, near Nineveh, that was traditionally associated with Jonah. Such colossal figures guarded entrances to palaces and protected their inhabitants.

CHAPTER 2

ANCIENT EGYPT

Giant statues of Ramesses II adorn the rock-cut façade of the Great Temple at Abu Simbel. Scenes at the temple show a plethora of gods and goddesses and Ramesses performing various sacred rites.

The Intellectual and Historical Setting

The River Nile was the lifeline of Ancient Egypt. Some Egyptian myths incorporated features of myths from neighboring cultures. Remnants of Egyptian myths can still be found in Christian or Muslim stories from Egypt.

A ncient Egypt was a land of many gods and goddesses. They ruled over all aspects of life and over the cosmos. Most of these gods and goddesses could take a variety of forms, depending on how a particular deity was perceived locally and which of its powers were invoked. The various functions of the gods in their different guises, and their relationships with each other, are described in myths.

Unlike other cultures, the Egyptians did not write down the stories about their gods in coherent narratives until comparatively late. Much of what is known about Egyptian deities comes from brief,

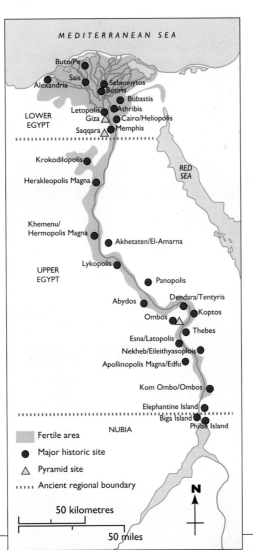

oblique references in religious texts fixed on the walls of tombs, coffins, and temples, or from associated rituals.

Oral tradition

The lack of a coherent written mythology suggests that these stories were mostly transmitted orally, giving the narrator or performer freedom of interpretation. Without a sacred canon, the myths could be adapted for different purposes, whether rituals, prayers, or magical spells. Keeping the myths "fluid" in this way accorded with the specifically Egyptian form of divine syncretism, which allowed the fusing of two or more gods along with their functions and powers.

The Pyramid Texts, which were hewn into the stone walls in the pyramid tombs of kings from the late 5th to the 8th dynasties, allude to most of the myths known from later periods. These texts together with their successors, the Coffin Texts of the Middle Kingdom, inscribed on the coffins of nobles, are the main source of Egyptian myths before more coherent stories appeared. Other major sources are the texts and representations of kings and gods found in temples.

Rejection and resurgence

In the 18th dynasty, King Amenhotep IV, who changed his name to Akhenaten, rejected all gods but Aten—the solar disk. Akhenaten tried to eliminate the myths that surrounded the old gods, but ultimately failed. His successors, among them the child-king Tutankhamen, reinstated all the old deities.

Most myths survived until the end of the ancient Egyptian religion. During that time, they came under the influence first of Christianity, from the 1st century A.D., and then, after 642 A.D., of Islam. Some myths were expanded or adapted to reflect changed political, economic, or religious circumstances.

Gods, Sacred Animals, and Myths

MYTHS, GODS, AND POLITICS
Like the Egyptian pantheon, Egypt's myths were concerned with two principal domains: creation and the workings of the cosmos; and social and political relations—especially those affecting the royal succession.

The stories explain how gods and cultic places acquired their names, what were their functions and how individual kings came to the throne. Often the cosmic and political domains overlapped. For example, aspects of Egypt's administration were transposed onto the celestial sphere, where the Moon god Thoth could appear as the "vizier" of the Sun god Re. Likewise the Egyptian pharaoh was imbued with certain cosmic qualities, and considered to be Re's "deputy" or "successor" (*seti*) on Earth.

With the unification of Upper (southern) and Lower (northern) Egypt in about 3000 B.C. came an increase in the number of ways the gods were represented. Early images from this period show the king with powerful animals as symbols on standards, or as his helpers in scenes of war or hunting.

The most common animal deities are the jackal Khontamenti ("Foremost of the Westerners," that is, the dead); the falcon, who represents the royal god Horus and personifies the living king; the bull; and the lion or lioness. These images are found in all periods of ancient Egyptian history. Other important personifications of goddesses are the snake and the scorpion, which became the symbol of the goddess Selket.

Calling on the gods

Egyptians thus worshiped the forces that posed a danger to them. Wary of the creatures in their environment, they gave them human shape and prayed to them for their favor and their protection. However, many deities retained their animal heads as a symbolic expression of their nature and their power, while human-headed gods wore their symbol on their head as an ornament or a crown.

Gods dwelt both in the sky and in the underworld. Through prayers and rituals they could be summoned to inhabit a temple, statue, or sacred animal. That is why the Egyptians worshipped certain animals and embalmed them. They mummified ibises, which were sacred to the god Thoth, cats (sacred to Hathor-Bastet), crocodiles (sacred to Sobek), and rams (sacred to Khnum).

SOME EGYPTIAN DEITIES

At first, gods and goddesses were represented by animals. Later, they took on human form, with only the head of the animal remaining.

A drawing on papyrus shows Geb, the male Earth, lying beneath Nut, the female sky, who arches over him supported by her father Shu, the god of light and air. The day- and night-barques of the Sun god can be seen on Nut's back.

OSIRIS   **NEPHTHYS**

The Egyptian pantheon

The pantheon of gods that were worshiped throughout Egypt consisted of deities who played a major role in the cosmos or in the state. The principal god was the Sun god Re or Amun-Re—the "king of the cosmos"—who presided over the council of gods. He was born by the sky-goddess Nut every morning, and traveled across her belly in his barque.

Some gods that were worshiped throughout Egypt did not have a fixed genealogical relationship or position within the pantheon. Chief among these was Hapi, the god who personified the Nile floods, which were vital to Egypt's agricultural prosperity.

In different periods, the members of the pantheon varied slightly. However, it was mostly the names of the deities or the forms that they took that differed, rather than their substance or functions.

The deity's head would be shown with the animal's ears and nose but with human hair and carrying the appropriate symbol—a Sun, Moon, and so on, on top.

LOCAL DEITIES

As well as worshiping the gods of the state pantheon, people also worshiped traditional local deities or "town gods" (*netjeru niutiu*) who were important to their area in terms of its landscape, its history or local community needs.

Thus, villages in the vicinity of desert depressions tended to have as their local gods lion deities, such as Pakhet ("She who tears apart"), or jackal deities, such as Wepwawet ("The opener of ways"), because these animals were recognized as dangerous. Jackal gods typically presided over the necropoles, the "cities of the dead" located in the desert regions. The two principal gods of the "underworld"—Khontamenti and the embalmer Anubis—were jackal gods.

Other common forms included snakes, such as Renenutet ("Nourishing Snake") in charge of the harvest; bull—aggressive and fertile gods such as Kem-Wer ("The Great Black One") of Athribis; and crocodile, such as Sobek ("Crocodile") of the oasis Fayyum. It is impossible to give the exact number of different deities that were worshiped in Egypt over its entire history.

SYNCRETISM—COMBINATIONS OF GODS

Egyptian gods could merge to form a new deity with different or extended functions and iconography.

The first part of the deity's name represented the dominant characteristic of the god, while the added names referred to more specific functions or features, which varied according to context. Thus, Re-Shu described the Sun god as the separator of sky and Earth by means of solar light—Shu being the god of light.

Shu-Onuris referred to Shu as "Bringer of the Distant One"—retriever of the solar Eye. The solar Eye was the distant lioness Hathor-Sakhmet, who angrily left her position at the forehead of Re.

Hathor-Tefnut-Sakhmet (-Bastet) was the complete personality of the solar Eye in its different aspects, combining Hathor as Sun disk with the fierce lioness Sakhmet or her appeased form, the cat Bastet.

SEKHMET

MESTERT

KHNUM

RE

The Sun God and his Family

The Sun god took three forms: the beetle Khepri ("He who comes into existence") in the morning, the falcon-headed Re during the day and, as the setting evening Sun, the human- or ram-headed Atum ("He who is complete"). Every morning, he had to fight the snake-god, and personification of chaos, Apophis. During the night the Sun traveled through the underworld, or interior of Nut, the sky-goddess, who swallowed Atum in the evening.

The opposite happened in the case of the many star-gods. They were born at night and swallowed by the sky-goddess in the morning. A short myth recounts how the Earth god, Geb, quarreled with Nut because she ate her own children. Geb was told not to worry, because all their children would reappear safe and sound the next evening.

The Moon god Thoth was the deputy, or vizier, of the Sun god, and also the messenger of the gods. He could appear as an ibis or baboon. In the myth of the quarrel between the divine brothers Horus and Seth, Thoth acted as judge.

Solar daughters

Another important cosmic deity was the daughter and "Eye" of Re. She personified the solar disk as the lioness Hathor-Tefnut, who was called Sakhmet ("The Powerful One") in her angry state, or Bastet ("She of Bubastis") in her friendly form of a cat. Hathor was also the goddess of love and music, and had a son, the child Moon god Ihy. She was one of the most important goddesses of the Egyptian pantheon, and had many manifestations and many names in the temples of Egypt.

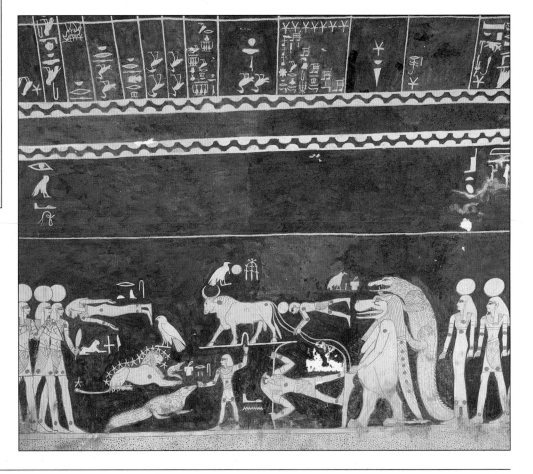

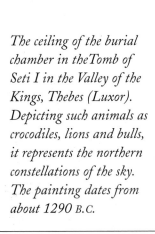

The ceiling of the burial chamber in the Tomb of Seti I in the Valley of the Kings, Thebes (Luxor). Depicting such animals as crocodiles, lions and bulls, it represents the northern constellations of the sky. The painting dates from about 1290 B.C.

The goddess Hathor of the west is depicted tending to "Horus of the two Horizons," Harakhte, the falcon-headed sky god.

Another solar daughter was called Maat. She represented justice, which was a most vital concept in the functioning of the Egyptian cosmos and state.

Order out of chaos

Egypt had several myths about the origins of the world, but these were ultimately very similar in structure. The variations are often due to local color.

The theme of the myths is mostly the creation of order out of an aquatic chaos, of differentiation out of unity. Cosmic order began with the first sunrise, and this solar creation was ritually repeated and celebrated each time a cycle—whether daily, monthly, yearly, or regnal—was completed. Creation was followed by death or destruction, and again by recreation, in an ever-recurring cycle.

A stone relief showing Isis and Osiris, from the Cushite culture in Ethiopia about 700 B.C. Egyptian myths spread far and wide.

CREATION MYTH

The most influential cosmogonic myth, originating from Heliopolis, involves many gods of the state-pantheon.

Atum, as the solitary creator-god, emerged from the primeval ocean Nun. From his seed, he created out of himself—that is, out of unity—duality in the form of the twins Shu, the god of light and air, and Hathor-Tefnut, the lioness personifying the solar disk. This couple begot the female sky, Nut, and the male Earth, Geb. They, in turn, produced the gods of the "Osiris cycle."

As the oldest son, Osiris inherited Geb's kingship. Osiris formed a pair with his sister Isis, who might originally have been the personification of the royal throne. She also personified the star Sirius. Osiris was often depicted as a mummified god with a crown expressing his role as ruler of the underworld. One of his manifestations was as the constellation Orion. Next, their brother Seth was born, who astronomically can be identified with both the Big Dipper constellation and the planet Mercury. His companion was his sister Nephthys (nebet hut, "Mistress of the House.")

Osiris was killed by Seth out of jealousy, but Isis managed to bear him a child after his death. She brought up their son, Horus, in secret, assisted by the snake Uto or Wadjit ("The Fresh/Green One") and the vulture Nekhbet ("She of El-Kab"), who each personified a royal crown.

Horus became king, and was equated with the living pharaoh. Horus' falcon-head and double crown refer to his nature as a sky-deity and manifestation of the morning star Venus on the one hand, and to his royal function on the other.

Struggle, Death, and Resurrection

The creation myth of Heliopolis provided the genealogical line for the living king, who was equated with the god Horus, the son and successor of Osiris.

The Osiris myth describes the struggle for royal power, which is a conflict between legitimate and illegitimate rule, between patrilineal and fratrilineal succession—whether the throne should be inherited by the son or brother of the deceased king. It also deals with death and resurrection, which relate to the cyclical decay and regrowth of the vegetation. Osiris comes to symbolize the Nile and hence the fertile land of Egypt, while his brother Seth is made the Lord of the desert and foreign countries.

The myth was also important for the beliefs concerning the afterlife. Every deceased person was later identified with Osiris as the dead and resurrected god, and was thus promised eternal life. The dead Osiris became the ruler of the underworld.

Horus avenges Osiris' death

In a dispute between Osiris and his brother Seth over the inheritance of Geb's kingship, Seth killed Osiris, dismembered the body and scattered the parts all over Egypt. This episode gave rise to the various cult-centers of Osiris, each one claiming to have a body-part as a relic.

After Osiris' murder, his sisters Isis and Nephthys traveled the land, collecting and

A statue of Isis nursing her son Horus, from the necropolis of Ballana or Qustul in Nubia. It dates from around 350–700 A.D.

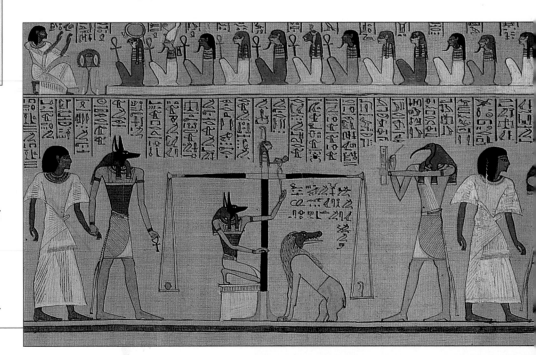

In the Book of the Dead *papyrus of Hunefer, a sequence shows Anubis leading in the deceased Hunefer; Anubis weighing his heart on a balance; Thoth recording the weight; then Horus presenting Hunefer to Osiris seated on the throne.*

reassembling their brother's body-parts, and managed to revive him briefly. This form of Osiris is called Wenenefer ("He who is well" or "complete.") Osiris' identification with the constellation Orion, which was invisible for approximately seventy days every year, explains the Egyptians' 70-day embalming rituals.

Isis, in the form of a harrier, hovered over the erect penis of Osiris, and conceived a son, Horus, whom she brought up in a reed-thicket to hide him from Seth. When Horus grew up, he set out to fight his uncle so as to avenge his father and gain legitimate rule.

THE PHARAONIC DIVINITY MYTH

Amun-Re, the king of gods, sees the queen of Egypt and finds her exceedingly beautiful. He takes on the appearance of her husband to seduce her. The queen conceives a child, which is to become the next king of Egypt. The child and its ka, one of the terms for the soul, are formed on Khnum's potter's wheel, and Amun-Re accepts the child as his own.

This myth thematizes the divine descent of the Egyptian pharaoh. Its original purpose was to legitimize Queen Hatshepsut's accession to the throne as pharaoh instead of her nephew, Thutmosis III. It was then copied by subsequent rulers and became a fixed part of royal ideology. Representations of the king's coronation by gods, or his being suckled by goddesses, served to reinforce the myth.

MYTH OF THE LOST SUN

The solar daughter, and Eye of the Sun god, Hathor-Tefnut (also called Sakhmet), fought with her father, Re, and left Egypt in anger. The loss of the Sun was a terrible problem for Egypt, and the goddess had to be persuaded to return. Hathor-Tefnut had retreated to Nubia, and her brother Shu, the god of light and air, and the Moon-god Thoth were dispatched to look for her.

When Shu and Thoth found the irate goddess, they used sistra (rattles made of faience or metal) and other musical instruments to turn the angry lioness Hathor-Tefnut-Sakhmet into the friendly, maternal cat Hathor-Bastet. Sistra and other rattling instruments, such as the menit, a collar of beads, were the typical cult objects of Hathor.

Upon her triumphant return to Egypt, the entire population rejoiced and celebrated with dancing and music. Hence the cult of Hathor was associated with music and dance. Hathor finally reached Memphis, the old capital, next to the city of Heliopolis, the center of the Sun cult.

This cosmic myth has been interpreted as describing the events leading up to the summer solstice—the day of the year when the Sun, which had previously been at its lowest (and most distant from the Earth), turns back to shine longer each day. However, the myth may also describe a simple daily interchange of Sun and Moon, with the Sun disappearing from view in the evening, and the Moon god being one of the deities that persuade the Sun to return to the sky. Generally, the Egyptians used episodes of the myth to describe any cosmic event that involved the absence of the Sun.

The boy king, Tutankhamon, stands before Nut, the sky goddess—from a wall painting in his tomb of 1327 B.C.

Temples, Statues, and Rituals

A sphinx, symbol of royal power and a form of the Sun god, sits before the 4,500-year-old pyramids at Giza.

Temples were seen as images of the cosmos. Their roofs represented the sky, their floors the underworld or primeval ocean, and their columns the vegetation.

The statues in temples were believed to be inhabited by the gods, and were fed and clothed daily by priests acting on behalf of the king. The daily ritual brought about the rebirth of the gods according to the model of the Sun god in his daily rising. All offerings were called the "Eye of Horus" (see panel opposite), evoking the mythic episode in which Seth gouged out Horus' eyes, which were later restored to him. The offerings were considered as essential to the well-being of the god as the Eye was to Horus.

Processions and rituals

Many festivals with religious and mythical significance took place in ancient Egypt. Often they included a procession of the local deities' cultic statues. Some involved rituals in which the cult-participants took on the role of mythical figures, making contact with the gods, who might issue oracles on such occasions.

INTO THE AFTERLIFE

Ancient Egyptians strived to ensure that the spirits of the dead would enjoy the afterlife. Pharaohs and wealthy civic leaders organized the construction of pyramids or tombs for themselves and arranged for funerals that would be grand and ostentatious. The mummy of the dead person traveled on a boat to the tomb on the west bank of the Nile, the location of the necropoles. Family visited the tomb regularly to make food offerings to their dead relation.

VITAL ORGANS
The dead person's lungs, liver, stomach, intestines and sometimes the heart were removed and placed in special jars and the body mummified. The jars were put in shrines that were carried to the tomb by priests.

FESTIVALS OF KARNAK
In the "Beautiful Festival of the Valley" in southern Egypt, the barque of Amun took the god from Karnak temple to Deir el-Bahari to spend the night in the temple of Hathor, who resided there as a solar cow-goddess. The population participated by celebrating in the tombs with its ancestors, dancing and presenting flowers. The festival ended with a feast of drinking, evoking the appeasement of the angry lioness and distant solar Eye. Annual visits to tombs to picnic with the ancestors still take place in Egypt today.

ANUBIS AND THE EYE OF HORUS
Many of the dead person's belongings, including furniture, clothes, and jewelry and other precious objects, were carried in boxes to the tomb to be buried with the body. The boxes were decorated with, among other things, images of Anubis and the Eye of Horus to watch over them in the afterlife.

THE COFFIN
The mummy was put in a painted coffin and placed inside a sarcophagus that was taken to the tomb on a boat atop a sledge. Along the way, priests sprinkled milk and incense and citizens paid their last respects.

THE TRIUMPH OF HORUS OVER SETH

As Osiris' son, Horus claimed the throne before the council of gods, but the All-Lord Atum considered Seth, Horus' uncle, to be the stronger candidate.

However, after Horus' mother, Isis, tricked Seth into admitting that the son should be given the inheritance, rather than a "stranger," the crown was given to Horus. The enraged Seth then challenged Horus to an underwater fight in the shape of two hippopotamuses. Later, Seth gouged out both of Horus's eyes and buried them on a mountain top where they grew into lotus-flowers. But Horus was healed by Hathor, who poured gazelle's milk into his eye-sockets.

In a new plot, Seth tricked Horus into coming to his house, where he tried to prove Horus' incompetence. However, Horus manged to turn round the situation to his advantage. When Seth appeared before the divine council to gloat about his victory and claim the kingship, the judge Thoth called for symbols of Seth and Horus to appear. Seth's symbol appeared from the depths of the water, while Horus' became a Moon disk that grew out of Seth's head. Thoth seized the disk and placed it on his own head as his divine symbol.

Finally, after another unsuccessful challenge by Seth, Osiris in the underworld was asked to judge between his son and his brother. Appalled by the unjust treatment of his son, Osiris threatened to carry off the gods to the underworld. This finally led to Horus' coronation as king. Seth, in fetters, acknowledged Horus' claim to the throne and—as compensation—was taken to the sky with Re, to become a god of thunder and storms. All the gods rejoiced at Horus becoming the new king.

The myth thematizes the problems of a just succession, but has also cosmic connotations, such as an explanation for the origin of the Moon disk.

The Omnipresence of Myths

The pyramids, built as mortuary monuments through many periods, were interpreted as primeval mounds from which the Sun arose, but also as a "ladders" to the sky for the soul of the deceased. Large wooden boats were buried next to several pyramids, to allow the deceased to travel in the sky like the Sun god.

Myths were omnipresent in all Egyptian society, in life as in death. They were evoked in prayers and hymns to the gods, in spells and curses, in medical remedies, as stories told for entertainment, and in everyday sayings.

An episode from the Osiris myth in which Isis protects her son Horus in the reed-thicket was frequently cited in magical spells and medical prescriptions. Everyday objects, such as jewelry, mirrors, cosmetic spoons, and headrests, were often in the shape of mythical beings.

In death, every person was identified with Osiris. The mummified corpse of the deceased would be attended by a priest posing as Anubis, the jackal-faced embalmer-god, while the wife of the deceased took on the role of Isis mourning her brother.

Egyptian mythology today

Several of the old Egyptian practices and beliefs survive in Egypt and its neighboring countries today. Thus, every Friday, women in Lower Nubia (Sudan) pour out libations at the tombs of relatives. This is a non-Muslim practice that replicates the cult of the dead Osiris. It is known from the Greco-Roman period, when a priestess in the role of Isis would make a weekly offering of drink to her dead husband.

In the Fayyum oasis in Egypt priests are paid in grain to recite prayers from the Koran every Friday at the grave of an ancestor, just like in ancient times when it was believed that priests would "transfigure" the dead with hymns and prayers. The belief in Osiris (and later Serapis) as

A tomb painting from about 80 B.C. shows Anubis preparing the body of Sennedjem for burial.

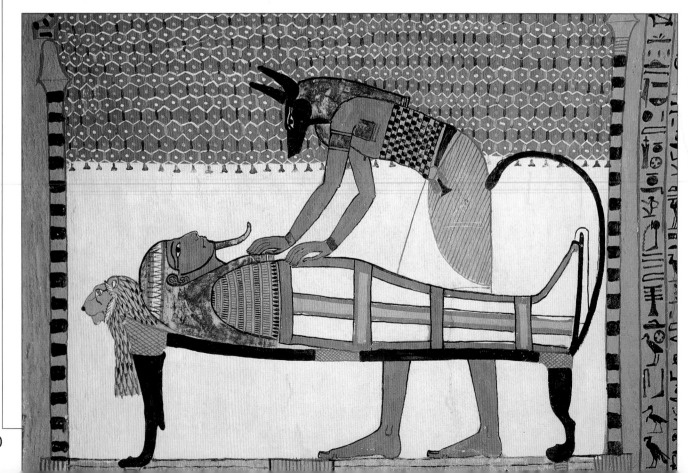

Lord of the Nile-flood survives among Coptic Christians in prayers to Christ as "ruler of the river."

The annual procession of the Muslim saint Abu el-Haggag around Luxor essentially continues the traditions of the ancient Opet festival. A statue of the saint is kept in the small mosque built in the first court of Luxor temple. Once a year it is taken out in a barque, like the images of the ancient Egyptian gods, and paraded through the town, accompanied by street entertainers and dancers.

In the western world, Egyptian mythical symbols influenced such great works of art as Mozart's *Magic Flute*, and continue to inspire and exercise the imagination of many creative artists, from painters and architects to film directors and advertising agents.

PREPARATION FOR THE AFTERLIFE

In ancient Egypt, it was believed that a person's soul would perish if it did not have its body to rest in. To stop the body decaying after death, it was made into a mummy. Embalmers took about 70 days to prepare the body for burial.

THE MUMMY
The dead body was opened, the vital organs were removed, and the corpse was packed in natron (soda) for 40 days to dry it out. Then the body was wrapped in linen bandages and shroud and tightly bound to keep its shape.

THE COFFIN
The wrapped mummy was placed in a wooden coffin. This surface of the coffin was highly decorated with symbols and icons of gods and goddesses and their mythical roles, and bore a mask of the dead person.

AMULETS AND MOULDS
The mummy was covered in protective amulets in shapes of characters or symbols from various myths. Common were Bastet-cats (Myths of the solar Eye), *udjat* ("healthy") Eyes (Contendings of Horus and Seth), and *djed* ("stability") pillars (Osiris-myth).

The story of Osiris's death and resurrection was also linked with the annual vanishing and return of the vegetation, which depended on the inundation of the Nile. Perforated moulds in the shape of the mummified Osiris called "Corn-Osiris" were filled with earth and seed, and watered until the seed sprouted. They symbolized the death and rebirth of the crops.

THE FINAL JOURNEY
The ancient Egyptians believed that a pharaoh, or king, was the son of the Sun god in this world. When the pharaoh died, he crossed from the land of the living to the land of the dead, where he was united with his father.

CANOPIC JARS
The internal organs of the body were placed in canopic jars, so-called because they resembled Osiris-Canopus, who was worshiped at the city of Canopus in the form of a human-headed jar. They were given the heads of four minor deities, the "Sons of Horus."

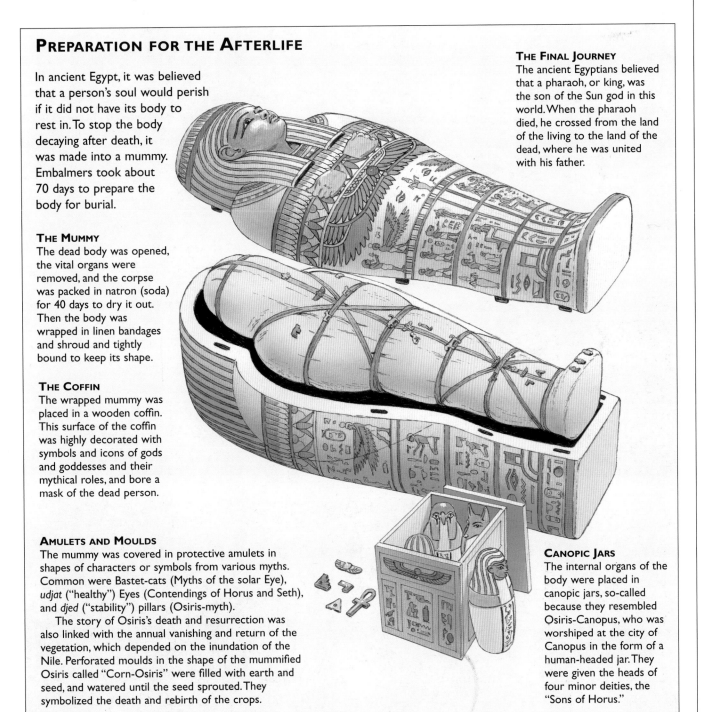

CHAPTER 3

Greece

The Parthenon on the Acropolis in Athens. The great temple was built between 447 and 432 B.C. The temple features an astonishing variety of sculpture on its pediments and metopes, depicting scenes and events relevant to the cult of the goddess Athena, such as the birth of the goddess and the Panthenaic procession.

Poetry and Mythology

The Greek world encircled the Aegean Sea and extended to the islands of Crete and Rhodes in the Mediterranean. The city-state of Athens was the cultural center and Mount Olympus, Greece's highest mountain, was the home of its chief deities.

The origins of Greek mythology are obscure. By the time Homer and Hesiod began composing their poems in the 8th century B.C., the myths that they related were already centuries' old—retold and reworked many times over by people in different parts of Greece to suit their own ethos.

The ancient Greek philosopher Aristotle defined *mythos*, Greek for "word" or "speech," as the plot of a literary work, in contrast to *logos*, also meaning "word," which connoted rational thought. It is through literature that most of the Greek myths have come to us.

Interpretations of myth

Homer's *Iliad* and *Odyssey*, composed orally before the advent of Greek writing, Hesiod's *Theogony*, the story of the creation of the universe, and the Homeric Hymns, poems written in Homeric style to honor the Olympian gods, are the primary sources of Greek myth. The tragedians of the "golden age" of Greece, the 5th century B.C., based their dramas on these ancient myths, while philosophers such as Empedocles and Plato offered new ways of understanding the tales, which served as both religious texts and artistic inspiration.

Extreme behavior

The tales of Greek mythology often deal with the extremes of behavior—deceit, lust, incest, murder, and even the eating of human flesh. Fantastic monsters and mythical journeys reflect both the perceptions of reality, as the Greeks colonized new lands and encountered new peoples and strange surroundings, and perceptions of the Greeks themselves.

Through mythology the Greeks continually reexamined their cultural principles and affirmed deeply held beliefs, such as the importance of justice, the strength of the human will, and the value of a strong society built upon laws and democracy.

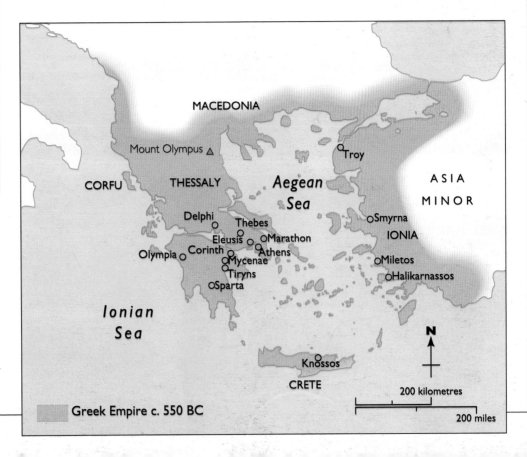

Greek Empire c. 550 BC

In the Beginning

In his *Theogony*, Hesiod tells how, out of Chaos (the void) sprang Gaia (the Earth), Tartaros (the Underworld), Eros (desire), Erebos (darkness), and Night. Night and Erebos produced Aither (high, clear air) and Day. Gaia by herself gave birth to Uranos (the sky), and together they bore the original divinities: the twelve Titans (giants with human form), three Cyclopes (one-eyed giants), and three Hekatonchires (creatures with 100 hands).

A family feud

After Uranos banished his offspring to Tartaros, Gaia persuaded Kronos, one of the Titans, to castrate his father and seize power. Kronos then married Rhea, his sister, who was also a Titan.

It had been foretold that one of Kronos' children would kill him, so he swallowed each child as it was born. For the sixth child, Zeus, Rhea substituted a stone, and secreted the baby with nymphs, who raised him.

When Zeus grew up, he attacked the Titans and defeated them in the *Titanomachy* (battle against the Titans). He forced Kronos to spew out his sisters and brothers and established himself as the king of the gods.

Goddess of wisdom

The goddess Athena emerged from the head of Zeus, fully formed. She carried a spear and shield and wore a crested helmet on her head, and an *aegis* (breastplate) featuring the head of Medusa, a snake-haired monster. Athena became the goddess of wisdom, and especially of strategy, cunning, and planning. She is associated with textile arts, such as weaving; ship-building, and industry; and military strategy. The owl, symbol of wisdom, was one of Athena's icons.

Athena and Poseidon competed to become the patron god of a new city in the district of Attica. Athena created the olive tree, whose fruit would provide the oil vital to cooking, lighting, and commerce, and was proclaimed the winner. The new city was named Athens in her honor.

A limestone statue of Zeus about to hurl a thunderbolt—from the Cyprus Museum, Nicosia. The statue was made in Cyprus in about 500 B.C.

The temple of Apollo at Delphi. Before the cult of Apollo, Delphi was the center of worship for Gaia and Themis (goddess of law or right), who was the second wife of Zeus.

Apollo and the Delphic Oracle

The shrine at Delphi was once guarded by the Python, a female dragon or serpent. When Apollo was only three days' old, he killed the Python with his bow and arrow after the creature went on a destructive rampage. The shrine at Delphi was then turned over to him. To honor the ancient goddesses who had held sway there in the past, Apollo called the priestess of his shrine the Pythia, a virgin who channeled the words of the god and spoke them to people seeking wisdom from the oracle.

ZEUS AND THE OLYMPIANS

With Zeus at their head, the twelve main Greek gods of the pantheon lived on Mount Olympus, the highest mountain in Greece, located in the north. They were called the Olympians. Another powerful god, Hades, a brother of Zeus, governed and dwelt in the Underworld.

Zeus The poet Hesiod called him the "father of gods and men, under whose thunder the broad Earth quivers."

Hera Goddess of marriage and family, and wife and sister of Zeus.

Apollo God of music, poetry, and medicine, the son of Zeus and the Titan Leto.

Athena Born from the head of Zeus, the goddess of wisdom as expressed by both military strategy and craft skills.

Hermes Messenger of the gods, the son of Zeus and Maia, a minor divinity, the patron of roads and commerce, protector of travelers.

Poseidon Ruler of the oceans, feared as the bringer of earthquakes.

Artemis Apollo's twin sister, virgin goddess of the hunt and of childbirth.

Ares God of war, son of Zeus and Hera.

Aphrodite Goddess of desire and procreation, wife of Hephaestus, who sprang from sea foam.

Hephaestus The lame god of the forge, son of Zeus and Hera.

Demeter Goddess of grain and agriculture.

Hestia Goddess of the hearth.

Hades God of the Underworld.

The Parthenon on the Acropolis in Athens. The great temple was built to honour Athena, after whom the city is named. "Parthenon" comes from the goddess's epithet parthenos, *meaning "virgin" in ancient Greek.*

Mortals and Gods

Herakles fighting with the centaur Eurytion. Herakles is said to have founded the Olympic Games.

H erakles (called Hercules by the Romans) was the greatest of the Greek mortal heroes, and the only one to take his place among the gods on Mount Olympus on his death. He was one of the earliest mythological figures to be depicted in Greek art, since the 8th century B.C., and the only hero to be worshiped throughout Greece. He was a man of extremes, enormously strong, enormously brave, and with enormous appetites. He once killed a savage lion that was slaughtering the flocks of King Thespius, and the king rewarded him by letting him sleep with his fifty daughters.

Herakles' story
Herakles was an illegitimate son of Zeus and Alcmene. When Hera, always jealous of her husband's infidelities, sent snakes to kill Herakles in his cradle, the infant, already superhumanly strong, strangled them. Hera later caused Herakles to go temporarily insane, and during the fit of madness he killed Megara, his beloved wife, and his own children. To atone for these terrible deeds, Herakles undertook twelve superhuman tasks (The Twelve Labors of Herakles), overseen by King Eurystheus.

Herakles met his death at the hands of his new wife, Deianeira. She was tricked by a centaur into smearing a poisonous mixture of blood and semen on his clothes, and the noxious mixture consumed his flesh. On his funeral pyre, Herakles was redeemed by the gods and, in a gesture of reconciliation, he married Hera's daughter Hebe and went to live in peace on Mount Olympus.

Prometheus and Pandora
Prometheus, son of a Titan, is said to have made the first humans (men) from dirt, containing the divine seed of Gaia,

PERSEUS AND ANDROMEDA
Perseus used magical weapons, obtained with the help of Athena, to cut off the snake-haired head of Medusa, one of the three Gorgons—monsters whose gaze turned people to stone. The winged horse Pegasus is said to have sprung to life when Medusa's blood hit the earth.

In Ethiopia, Perseus discovered the beautiful Andromeda chained to a rock, ready to be sacrificed to a sea monster because of a slight against the sea goddess Thetis. Perseus offered to rescue Andromeda in return for her hand in marriage. Perseus slew the sea creature, and the marriage feast followed immediately. After their deaths, Athena turned Perseus and Andromeda into constellations.

Head of Medusa as shown on a vase.

and water. Zeus, who had been tricked by Prometheus, decided to punish humanity by depriving men of fire. Men had learned to survive on cooked meat, and now began to starve, so Prometheus stole fire back by hiding it in a fennel stalk. Because fire symbolizes civilization, Prometheus has long been seen as the bringer of culture to humanity.

Zeus punished Prometheus by chaining him to a rock in the Caucasus mountains, where every day an eagle, emblem of Zeus, would eat his liver, which regrew every night. As a further punishment to men, Zeus ordered his son Hephaestus to fashion a woman, as yet unknown to the world, out of clay and bring her to life. This creature was called Pandora ("All-Gifted") since many of the gods gave her special gifts. Pandora, carrying a jar or box, was presented to men, and later opened the container and released evil and sickness into their world, retaining only hope so that humanity would not despair.

JASON AND MEDEA

Jason, prince of Iolcos, set sail on the *Argo*, with Herakles, Theseus and the musician Orpheus, to steal the Golden Fleece in the faraway kingdom of Colchis ruled by King Aeetes. The voyage was treacherous, and the heroes battled with monsters and faced many dangers, such as the Symplegades, the Clashing Rocks.

Medea, daughter of Aeetes and a sorceress, having fallen in love with Jason, used her magic to put the dragon guarding the Golden Fleece to sleep. To gain more time, she even killed her own brother Apsytrus, flinging the pieces of his dismembered corpse into the water to force her father to retrieve them in order to give his son a proper burial.

Jason returned to Iolcos with the Golden Fleece and Medea to discover that Pelias, his uncle, had killed his father, King Aeson, and his mother had killed herself out of grief. In revenge, Medea persuaded Pelias' daughters that they could rejuvenate their father in a magic bath, but after following her instructions, they only succeed in killing and cooking him. The people of Iolcos were outraged by this news, and forced Jason and Medea to take flight.

They fled to Corinth, where Jason decided to marry the local princess. Medea, beside herself with rage, poisoned the princess and her father, and in some versions of the story also killed her children by Jason. He, forlorn and bereft of his family and friends in Corinth, visited the decomposing hull of the *Argo* and was killed when a rotten beam fell on him.

The Trojan War

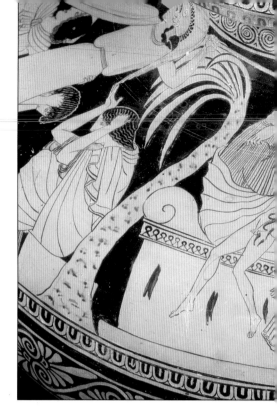

THE CITY OF TROY

Troy—also called Ilium or Ilion—was destroyed in approximately 1250 B.C. Archeologists have excavated a site in northwestern Asia Minor (now Turkey) and have determined that a prosperous city flourished there during the first half of the 13th century B.C. It is impossible to say whether that city really was Homer's Troy, or whether the Trojan War really took place, but certainly the ancient Greeks believed in its historicity, and the myth may well have some basis in fact.

The origins of the conflict between Greece and Troy are entrenched in myth. It was foretold that Paris, son of King Priam of Troy, would be the destroyer of Troy.

When, later, as a young man, Paris was chosen to decide which of the goddesses Hera, Athena or Aphrodite should be awarded a golden apple, each of them promised him something special if he would choose her. Aphrodite promised him the most beautiful woman in the world—Helen, wife of King Menelaus of Sparta—and he readily awarded the apple to the goddess of Love. Helen was the daughter of Leda and Zeus, after he had come to Leda in the form of a beautiful, amorous swan.

Paris traveled from Troy to Sparta, in Greece, and was welcomed into Menelaus' home as a guest. However, he violated the guest–host relationship, sacred in antiquity, by abducting Helen and sailing with her back to Troy (in some versions Helen goes willingly).

This breach of honor could not go unavenged, and so Agamemnon, King of Mycenae, sent out a call to all the kings and rulers of Greece to unite in arms to attack the city of Troy. Most came willingly, but two of the war's greatest heroes Odysseus and Achilles had to be cajoled.

The Greeks expected to defeat the Trojans quickly, but they were not prepared for the vast walls protecting the city and the courage and tenacity of its people. The Greeks also experienced internal struggles in their ranks when Agamemnon seized Achilles' woman, Briseis, and the furious Achilles withdrew from the fighting.

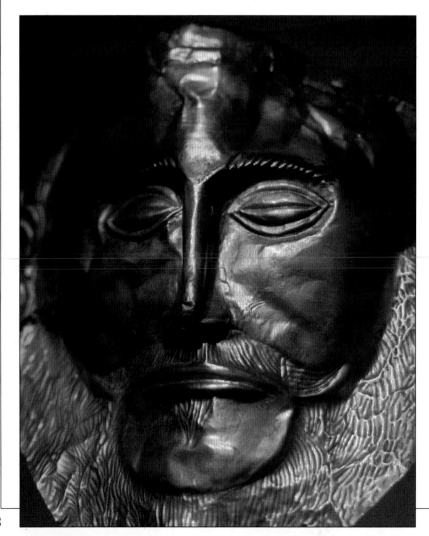

The so-called "Mask of Agamemnon", discovered at Mycenae. It is now known that the gold-leaf death mask predates Agamemnon by some 300 years.

A vase depicting Neoptolemus, son of Achilles, slaughtering Priam, who has taken refuge on an altar.

ODYSSEUS

Homer's *Odyssey* tells the story of Odysseus' perilous ten-year journey home after the Trojan War. Blending elements of martial epic with the monsters and magic of folklore, the *Odyssey* presents the timeless story of a man trying to readjust to civilian life after years at war.

Athena, always attracted to men of cunning, protected and guided Odysseus, whom Homer called "the man of many ways," through his many adventures. Odysseus encountered Polyphemus the Cyclops, a one-eyed giant, the sea monsters Skylla and Charybdis, the witch Circe (aunt of Medea), and the Sirens, seductive hybrid creatures who lured sailors to their deaths upon the rocks with their songs. Odysseus even journeyed to the Underworld, where he met Agamemnon and Achilles, the latter having traded a long but quiet life for a short but glorious one.

When Odysseus finally reached Ithaka, his homeland, he found that his wife, Penelope, had been besieged by 108 suitors who wanted to marry her and take control of the kingdom. With the help of his son Telemachus and his faithful retainers, Odysseus, disguised as a humble beggar, defeated the suitors in an archery contest, which ended in a bloody battle.

It is at this point, in the 10th year of the war, that Homer's epic the *Iliad* begins. Without Achilles, the Greeks faltered in battle, suffering heavy losses at the hands of the Trojans. Patroclus, Achilles' closest friend, was killed by the great Trojan warrior Hector, son of Priam and Hecuba, and Paris' elder brother. Patroclus had gone into battle wearing Achilles' armor to inspire fear in the Trojan lines.

Achilles, half-mad with grief and guilt at the news, returned to the fighting. Three times he pursued Hector around the walls of Troy, before killing him. He then lashed the corpse to his battle chariot and dragged it around the camp. However, the gods supported Priam in his quest to give his son a proper burial. Paris eventually killed Achilles, after shooting him in the heel, his one weak spot, with an arrow.

The long war ended when Odysseus devised the stratagem of the Trojan Horse. The finest Greek warriors hid inside the massive, hollow horse while the other Greeks sailed away as if in defeat. The Trojans, believing the horse to be an

This terracotta cup from c.490 B.C. shows Eos, winged goddess of dawn, with the dead body of her son Memnon, killed by Achilles in the Trojan War.

offering to the gods that the Greeks had left behind, dragged it inside their city walls. At night, as the Trojans slept off their celebratory drinking, the Greeks emerged from the horse, attacked and burned the city and enslaved the women.

CHRONOLOGY OF THE TROJAN WAR

1600–1200 B.C.
Mycenaean culture flourishes (Late Bronze Age).
1250 B.C.
Destruction of Troy.
1200–800 B.C.
The Dark Ages.
750 B.C.
Homer composes the *Iliad* and *Odyssey*.

Deities, Cults, and Temples

"The Abduction of Persephone," by Italian Baroque sculptor Gian Lorenzo Bernini.

The myth of Demeter and Persephone is the story of the changing seasons. Persephone was the daughter of Demeter, the goddess of agriculture, by Zeus, who was Demeter's brother. One day, Persephone disappeared, abducted by Hades, god of the Underworld, who took her down to his kingdom. For nine days, the grief-stricken Demeter roamed the Earth in search of her daughter. On the tenth day, after Helios, the Sun, informed her that Zeus had sanctioned Hades' act, Demeter left Mount Olympus, vowing to wander the Earth for ever.

Disguised as an old woman, she arrived in Eleusis, where the daughters of King Celeus welcomed her. She remained in the household as a nurse to Queen Metaneira's baby, Demophoon, whom she planned to make immortal by putting him into the fire every night to burn away his mortal elements. When Metaneira discovered Demeter performing this ritual, she was horrified. Demeter revealed her true identity, telling the queen that now her son would remain mortal for ever.

The arrival of winter

Continuing to roam, Demeter ignored her duties and no crops were allowed to grow. Zeus, out of mercy for the starving people on Earth, intervened: Persephone would be allowed to spend two-thirds of the year on Earth with her mother, but, because she had consumed some pomegranate seeds (a symbol of marriage), she would have to return to spend one-third of the year below with Hades. While Persephone was away in the Underworld, Demeter mourned, the Earth grew cold and barren and winter was created.

ANCIENT GREEK TEMPLE
The greatest representation of Greek architecture and art is the temple, *naos* in ancient Greek. The pediments and friezes of monumental temples, like the Parthenon, often depicted battles between gods and heroes (representing civilization) and monsters and giants (representing chaos and disorder).

TENEMOS
The sacred site on which the temple was built was called the *tenemos*, and was often indicated by a tenemos-wall, a rock, and a tree. Sacred sites were where people believed sacred forces flowed, as at a spring or well. The olive tree, gift of Athena as patron of Athens, stood on the Acropolis, providing shade and beauty and marking the site as a holy area.

SACRIFICE

Sacrifice was the most important aspect of Greek religious practice. A sacrificial animal was led to the altar, its throat was cut, the blood was collected, small portions of meat, fat, and bones were burned for the gods, and the rest of the meat was eaten by the celebrants.

OFFERINGS AT THE ALTAR

The altar was the most essential feature of the Greek temple. It was constructed of plain rocks or of white-washed brick or hewn stones and stood outside the temple, facing to the east. Worshipers stood around the altar while sacrifices to the gods were burned on the sacred flame.

THE UNDERWORLD

The Greeks believed that the souls of the dead passed into the Underworld, known as Hades, which was also the name of Zeus' brother who reigned there. Hermes in his role as *psychopomp* (escort of souls) would lead dead souls, after a proper burial, to the Underworld.

In the Underworld, the ferryman Charon, in exchange for a few coins put in the mouth or on the eyelids of the deceased during burial, would take the souls across the infernal rivers. These included the Styx (river of Hate) and Lethe (river of Forgetfulness, from which the word 'lethal' is derived). In Hades, certain regions—Erebus and Tartarus—were reserved for those sentenced to eternal punishment.

Among these was Tantalus, who was condemned to starve forever although only just out of reach of water and fruit (hence the English word 'tantalize'). Brave warriors, however, could count on spending eternity in the Elysian Fields or the Islands of the Blessed Dead.

HOUSEHOLD GODS

Religious worship also took place at home as well as in temples. Hestia, the goddess of the hearth, was the guardian of the household. She is not associated with many myths, because her place in Greek religion was private rather than public, but she was important to family ceremonies. Hermes, the intermediary between gods and humans, also served as a protector of households and streets. Columns called "herms," featuring the head of the god on top, were common.

GODDESS OF THE HUNT

Artemis, the twin sister of Apollo, was the virgin goddess of the hunt. She cruelly punished any man attempting to compromise her chastity. When the hunter Actaeon saw her bathing in the woods, she turned him into a deer and he was torn apart by his own dogs. Another hunter, Orion, threatened to rape her, so she summoned up a scorpion from the ground which stung both Orion and his dog to death. Orion became a constellation, and his dog turned into Sirius, the Dog Star. The young girls worshipped Artemis at her temple at Brauron by wearing bear costumes and dancing, in a rite of passage undertaken before marriage.

PRIESTS AND MUSICIANS

Greek priests or priestesses monitored the sacred *tenemos* and ensured that it was not profaned, assisted in sacrifices and served as treasurers of the temples. Musicians with lyres and flutes accompanied the singing of sacred hymns.

THE STATUE OF THE GOD

In the 5th century B.C., large-scale marble sculptures of the gods were situated in the main chamber inside the temple, facing the doors, which stood open during the burning of the sacrifice. The temple housed both the cult image of the god and his property, but actual worship took place outside the temple itself.

Plays, Playwrights, and Theaters

The first of the great Greek tragedians was Aeschylus. His trilogy of plays called *Oresteia*, or "Story of Orestes," was first performed in 458 B.C. It tells the story of Agamemnon's death on his return from Troy, and of his son Orestes.

Agamemnon was descended from Tantalus, who cooked up his own son Pelops to serve to the gods. Agamemnon's father, Atreus, was doomed to repeat the sins of his ancestors. After Atreus' brother Thyestes had committed adultery with his wife Aerope, Atreus feigned reconciliation and invited his brother to a banquet at which he served the cooked flesh of Thyestes' own sons. With these grave crimes lurking in the past, the family of Agamemnon was supremely dysfunctional. However, Aeschylus' trilogy seeks a path of redemption and justice, and demonstrates that the gods, like humans, can grow and mature.

Murder, revenge, and reconciliation

In the first play of the trilogy, Agamemnon's wife, Clytemnestra, plots vengeance against her husband for having sacrificed their daughter Iphigenia to Artemis before the Trojan War. Pretending to welcome Agamemnon back as her husband and king, Clytemnestra murders him with an ax (or a sword) as he bathes. At the end of the play, she exults in her revenge and triumph, ignoring warnings that her son, Orestes, will return to avenge his father's death. In the second play, Orestes kills his mother, but is then besieged by the Furies, horrible monsters visible only to him.

The final play of the trilogy, called the *Eumenides* ("The Kindly Ones"), is symbolic of the beginnings of the Athenian system of justice. Orestes is acquitted of matricide, and the Furies are changed into the Eumenides, to become a force of peace and goodness for humanity.

A lasting legacy

Greek mythology was a constant source of fascination to the writers and artists of the Renaissance, and it continues to inspire and enthrall us today.

In its stories of creation, its tales of adventure and heroism, and its gods of fertility, rebirth, and justice, Greek mythology seems to shares a common ancestry with the folklore and myth of other archaic cultures, such as Mesopotamia, India, and Egypt.

"Oedipus and the Sphinx," a painting by 19th-century French artist Jean Auguste Dominique Ingres.

ELEMENTS OF GREEK THEATER

Theater was a central part of life in ancient Greece. During the 5th century B.C., theatrical festivals were held twice a year in Athens and in the countryside.

Dedicated to Dionysus, who was said to have invented tragedy, Athens' Dionysia and Leneia festivals were held in the Theater of Dionysus on the southern slope of the Acropolis. The theater could hold 16,000 spectators. Dramatists used tales from mythology for their plots, often reinterpreting them for dramatic effect. Actors wore masks, long robes, and buskins (platform shoes so they could be seen better).

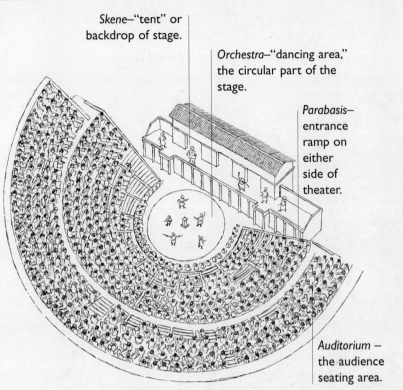

Skene—"tent" or backdrop of stage.

Orchestra—"dancing area," the circular part of the stage.

Parabasis—entrance ramp on either side of theater.

Auditorium – the audience seating area.

The ancient theater at Epidauros in the Peloponnese is still used today. The acoustics are as good as in any high-tech theater.

However, the Greek tales of gods and heroes, although rooted in antiquity, are still relevant to the modern psyche. In his book *The Power of Myth*, Joseph Campbell sums up why these myths remain so pertinent to us today.

"These bits of information from ancient times, which have to do with the themes that have supported human life, built civilizations, and informed religions over the millennia, have to do with deep inner problems, inner mysteries, inner thresholds of passage, and if you don't know what the guidelines are along the way, you have to work it out for yourself. But once this subject catches you, there is such a feeling, from one or another of these traditions, of a deep, rich, life-revivifying sort that you don't want to give it up."

THE STORY OF OEDIPUS

Oedipus Tyrannos, by the Greek playwright Sophocles, was first performed around 425 B.C. Oedipus is the archetypal tragic hero in a play that centers on human attempts to avoid fate.

Jocasta, wife of Laius, the king of Thebes, bears a son, who, it is prophesied, will one day murder his father and marry his mother. In fear, Laius abandons the infant on a hillside after piercing his ankles and binding them with a thong (Oedipus means "swollen foot.") However, the baby is rescued by a shepherd and raised by the king of Corinth as his own.

When Oedipus reaches manhood and learns of the prophecy, he leaves Corinth to avoid fulfilling his destiny. Outside Thebes, he encounters a stranger on the road and kills him after an argument.

He arrives at the city to learn that the Thebans have been terrorized by the Sphinx, a hybrid female monster who devours anyone that fails to solve her riddle. Oedipus, however, succeeds, and the Sphinx is so mortified that she throws herself off a cliff. Oedipus then becomes the ruler of Thebes and marries the queen, Jocasta.

One day, a messenger from Corinth informs Oedipus that his "father" has died. Oedipus is relieved that he has managed to avoid his terrible fate, after all. But when the messenger tells him that he was adopted, Jocasta, his mother and wife, realizing the dreadful truth, hangs herself.

Oedipus, devastated by this and by the weight of his realizations, tears out his eyes and goes into exile.

CHAPTER 4

ROME

*The ruins of the Temple of Mars Ultor
("Mars the Avenger") built in the center
of the Forum Augustum to commemorate
Augustus' victory over Brutus and
Cassius, the assassins of Julius Caesar.
The temple contained statues of Mars
and Venus, as well as of Julius Caesar.*

Gods of the Empire

CERES
Ceres, whose name gives us "cereal," was the goddess of grain and the fertility of nature. She was connected with the Roman Earth goddess Tellus, who was equivalent to the Greek Gaia.

During a famine at the end of the 5th century B.C., the Sibylline books, a source of prophecy for the Romans, recommended that the Romans worship Ceres, Liber and Proserpina. (respective Roman counterparts of the Greek deities Demeter, Dionysus, and Persephone).

A temple to these three stands on the Aventine Hill in Rome. Romans would sacrifice to Ceres after a funeral, to purify their homes, since her daughter had associations with Hades—the world of the dead.

T he Roman Empire dominated most of what is now modern Europe from 27 B.C., when Augustus became the first emperor, until the 4th century A.D. The Romans absorbed and adapted much of Greek mythology through the Etruscans, an ancient Italian civilization, but they focused more on war and agriculture.

Ceres, the Roman goddess equivalent to the Greek Demeter, and Mars, the Roman Ares, became the most important figures in their pantheon. As Rome expanded its borders, it incorporated numerous elements of religion and mythology from widely diverse cultures, from Egypt and Greece to the Celts in the north, and associated them with their own mythology.

History and legend

The Romans also included several historicized legends in their mythology. Authors such as the historian Livy (59 B.C.–17 A.D.), the poet Virgil (70–19 B.C.), and the Greek biographer and historian Plutarch (c. 46–126 A.D.) treated the founders of Rome, the twins Romulus and Remus, as historical people.

Mars

Although Mars became associated with Ares, the Greek god of war, he was originally an ancient Italic god of agriculture: the guardian of fields and boundaries. Among the Celts, Mars was a protector and healer as well as a god of war.

Temples and altars to Mars are found in Rome and all over Italy. The *Ara Martis* (Altar of Mars) was located in the Campus Martius in Rome and was served by a priest known as the *flamen Martialis*. There are other temples to Mars on the Via Appia (Appian Way) just outside Rome, in the Circus Flaminius and in the Forum of Augustus, also called the Forum of Mars.

Augustus built his temple to Mars Ultor, "Mars the Avenger," in 42 B.C. to commemorate the defeat of Brutus and Cassius, the assassins of Julius Caesar, at the Battle of Philippi. The month of March is named after Mars.

The Roman empire during the reign of Augustus 27 B.C.–14 A.D. Rome was the sacred center. The Romans accepted into their religion the gods and goddesses of the countries they conquered and ruled.

ROMAN PANTHEON

ROMAN NAME	GREEK NAME
JUPITER, JOVE	ZEUS
JUNO	HERA
NEPTUNE	POSEIDON
MARS	ARES
APOLLO	APOLLO
DIANA	ARTEMIS
CERES	DEMETER
MERCURY	HERMES
BACCHUS, LIBER	DIONYSUS
MINERVA	ATHENA
VENUS	APHRODITE
VULCAN	HEPHAESTUS
VESTA	HESTIA
CUPID	EROS
SATURN	KRONOS
TELLUS	GAIA

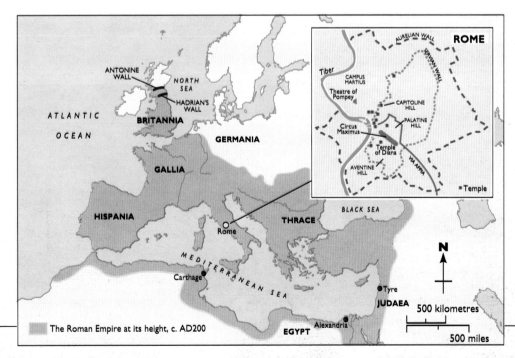

The Roman Empire at its height, c. AD200

Birth of an Empire

THE FIRST ROMAN WOMEN
Romulus attracted men to his new city of Rome by offering sanctuary to refugees, but no women came. Romulus devised a plan: he would host a festival for the Italic agricultural god Consus and would invite all the neighbors.

The Sabines, a nearby people, came to the festival along with their women and children. On a signal from Romulus, the young men of Rome snatched all the young Sabine women and carried them off. By the time the Sabines had prepared an army to fight the Romans, the women had already married the Roman men and borne them children.

"Dido receiving Aeneas and Cupid disguised as Ascanius," by Italian artist Solimena from the 1720s.

The Roman poet Virgil, in his final work, the *Aeneid*, used the themes of Homer's *Iliad* and *Odyssey* to tell the story of the founding of Rome by the Trojan Aeneas. The son of King Anchises and the goddess Venus, Aeneas came to represent the greatness of Rome and the monumental struggle to establish the vast and powerful Roman Empire. Through his hero Aeneas, Virgil aimed to show that even though Rome's past was filled with violence and conquest, the *Pax Augusta* (The Peace of Augustus) was the fulfilment of a great destiny.

From Troy to a new land

Aeneas fled the burning city of Troy carrying his father on his shoulders, his household gods in his arms, and leading his son Ascanius by the hand. This potent image became the symbol of Roman piety, representing filial duty, devotion to the gods, and care for future generations. Aeneas' wife, Creusa, following behind, was lost in the confusion, but still Aeneas had to press on.

The first half of the *Aeneid* mirrors Homer's *Odyssey*. Aeneas, bewildered and uncertain of his destiny but ordered by the gods to forge ahead, sailed with his crew and encountered many of the same monsters that Odysseus faced in his adventures. Like Odysseus, he visited the Underworld in his search for answers. While there he was shown the future of Rome and what his destiny would bring.

When the Trojans reached the North African city of Carthage, Aeneas fell in love with the queen, Dido, but the force of his destiny would not allow him to settle there. At last Aeneas landed on the coast of Italy and realized that this land held his destiny. Unfortunately, indigenous people already lived there, and Aeneas had to fight for the land.

The Latins, led by the heroic Turnus, fought to defend their country but, in a scene that recalls the duel between

Achilles and Hector in the *Iliad*, Aeneas killed Turnus and established the beginnings of Rome.

Dido's story

After Dido's brother murdered her husband, Sychaeus, in their homeland of Phoenicia, Dido fled to the northern coast of Africa. There she founded the city of Carthage, which was thriving by the time the hero Aeneas and his crew arrived.

Dido had sworn a vow of perpetual fidelity to her dead husband, but Venus sent her son Cupid to make Dido fall in love with Aeneas, another of Venus's sons. While Dido was showing Aeneas her city from a hilltop, a storm forced them to take shelter in a cave, where they made love. Dido believed that this was a divine wedding. However, Jupiter sent Mercury down to urge Aeneas to continue on to Italy to fulfil his destiny. As his ship sailed away, Dido killed herself with Aeneas' sword while lying on her funeral pyre. In the Underworld, Aeneas met Dido again, now reunited with her husband. She refused to speak to Aeneas.

Symbol of menace

Julius Caesar and the subsequent emperors of Rome traced their lineage back through Aeneas to Venus, establishing themselves as divine by birth. It became customary for emperors to be deified and worshiped after their deaths.

To the Romans, the story of Dido symbolized two major threats to the Roman state: Hannibal, ruler of Carthage from 247–183 B.C., who almost conquered Italy with his elephants; and Cleopatra, Queen of Egypt, who bore a son to Julius Caesar and fought with Marc Antony against Augustus at the Battle of Actium in 31 B.C.

This relief on a stone altar from about 150 A.D. shows the shepherd Faustulus finding the she-wolf and Romulus and Remus.

THE TWIN FOUNDERS OF ROME

Ascanius, the son of the hero Aeneas, founded the city of Alba Longa on the coast of Italy. In later generations, a woman of Alba Longa, Rhea Silva, gave birth to twin sons after being raped by Mars. Her uncle the king ordered that the illegitimately-born infants be left on the banks of the river Tiber to die. However, a she-wolf nursed the baby boys, called Romulus and Remus, until they were discovered and adopted by a shepherd.

When the boys grew up, they decided to found a city on the site where the she-wolf suckled them and saved their lives. But they argued about the exact location. In the end, Romulus murdered his brother and called the city "Roma" after himself.

The "She-Wolf," a bronze statue from Rome, c. 500 B.C. The suckling babies were added in the 15th century and were recently removed.

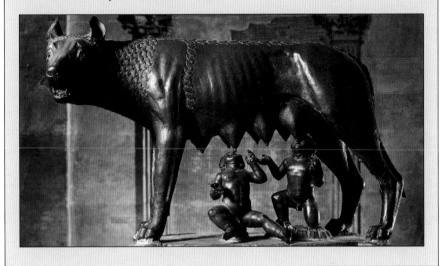

Seduction, Suicide, and Revenge

DON'T LOOK BACK
Orpheus was the most famous mortal musician, whose songs could charm even the trees. On Orpheus' wedding day, his wife, Eurydice, stepped on a snake and died from its venomous bite.

In his grief, Orpheus was driven to descend to the Underworld to ask Persephone and Hades to return Eurydice to him. His song was so moving that all the inhabitants of Tartarus, in the depths of the Underworld, wept when they heard it. The king and queen of the Underworld agreed to his request, provided that he did not turn around to look at Eurydice until they had reached the world of the living again. But Orpheus could not resist the temptation to glance behind him to make sure that she was following. Eurydice was snatched back into Hades for ever.

The *Metamorphoses* by the Roman poet Ovid (43 B.C.–17 A.D.) is one of the most influential and important sources of Greco-Roman mythology. These tales of transformation recount the lusts and loves of the gods and the helplessness of human beings (especially females) in the face of divine forces.

The loves of Jupiter

Jupiter, known for his sexual appetites, changes his form to seduce attractive mortal women. He appears as a bull to Europa, a swan to Leda, a cloud to Io, and shower of gold to Danae. Some of his lovers do not fare well after their encounters with the king of the heavens. Io, for instance, is transformed into a lovely cow and remains in bovine form for years. Callisto, a young huntress devoted to the virgin goddess Diana, is turned into a bear after being raped by Jupiter and giving birth to a son, Arcas. Both mother and son end up as constellations.

Doomed lovers

A young man called Pyramus loved a young woman, Thisbe, who lived next door, but their fathers forbade them to marry. The lovers agreed to slip out at night and meet under a white mulberry tree outside the city.

Thisbe arrived first, and while she waited, a lioness fresh from a kill approached to drink from a nearby spring. Thisbe fled in fright to the shelter of a

A Roman mosaic from a villa in Sicily from the 3rd century B.C. shows hunters paying homage to Diana, goddess of hunting, at a sacrificial fire.

cave, dropping her white cloak in the process. The lioness began to maul the cloak with her bloody paws, eventually leaving it on the ground.

When Pyramus came upon the bloodied cloak of his beloved, he thought her dead, and in his grief plunged his sword into his side. Thisbe emerged from her hiding place, realized what had happened, fell upon her lover's sword, and died beside him. The fountain of their blood caused the white fruit of the mulberry to be stained dark purple. This story is best known to us from Shakespeare's *A Midsummer Night's Dream*, and echoes the plot of *Romeo and Juliet*.

A sister's revenge

Tereus and Procne were happily married, but Procne missed her sister Philomela, whom she had not seen since the wedding. She asked her husband to fetch Philomela for a visit.

When Tereus saw Philomela, he was seized by desire for her. Having brought her to his home shores, he attacked Philomela, and when she would not cease her loud praying and cursing, he cut out her tongue. He then imprisoned her in a small stone cabin not far from his palace, telling Procne that Philomela had died on the journey.

While Procne mourned for her sister, Philomela spent her days weaving the story of her misfortune into an elaborate tapestry, which she had an old serving woman deliver to the queen. Procne understood everything upon seeing it. She released her sister and as revenge upon her faithless husband, cut up her own son Itys and served him for dinner. All three were changed into birds with red breasts and crests to symbolize the violence and bloodshed of their story.

Thisbe and Pyramus—in a floor mosaic from the House of Dionysus in Paphos, Cyprus, built in the 2nd century A.D.

UNLUCKY IN LOVE

Apollo made fun of Cupid's small bow and arrows, arrogantly asserting that he, Apollo, god of archery, was much more powerful. Apollo loved Daphne, a river nymph, so Cupid decided to teach him a lesson. Cupid used his arrow of passion on Apollo and then shot a lead arrow, which deadened desire, into Daphne.

As Apollo pursued the nymph, she prayed to be kept a virgin always, like the goddess Diana, and was changed into the laurel tree. Apollo caressed the newly formed bark covering Daphne's torso, vowing to make the laurel his sacred tree and make the laurel wreath the symbol of triumph for victorious Roman generals.

Apollo also loved a boy, Hyacinthus, and even abandoned his oracle at Delphi to spend time hunting and exercising with the boy. But one day, as they played at throwing the discus, Hyacinthus was struck on the head and died. From his blood and white skin sprang the hyacinth.

Baroque sculptor Bernini's marble statue of Apollo and Daphne, an interpretation of classical Roman mythology.

Pagans and Christians

*The Temple of Vesta in
Rome, which housed the
Vestal Virgins. Vesta was
the goddess of the hearth.*

The Romans held numerous *feriae* ("holidays" or "festivals") throughout the year in honor of their gods. Each holiday included prayers, sacrifices, and rituals, performed by priests outside the temple or shrine of the particular god being honored. Everything had to be carried out perfectly lest the god's anger be stirred.

For most Romans the *feriae* meant a day off work. The Saturnalia, festival of Saturn, was an occasion of unrestrained freedom. It was celebrated between 17 and 23 December, at the time of the winter solstice. On that one day of the year, people could gamble in public, and often masters served their slaves.

Many Roman festivals, such as the Lupercalia, were later incorporated into the Christian calendar. The Lupercalia was an ancient purification and fertility festival celebrated on 15 February. In 494 A.D., Pope Gelasius converted it to the Festival of the Purification of the Virgin Mary. The birthday of Sol, the Sun god, on 25 December, was later made to coincide with the birthday of Jesus.

THE LUPERCALIA ON THE PALATINE HILL
The Lupercalia started at the Lupercal cave, located at the foot of the Palatine Hill. The festival was riotous and popular.

MYSTERIOUS ORIGINS
The Palatine Hill is where Romulus and Remus were said to have been suckled by the she-wolf.

The Lupercalia seems to have combined rituals of purification and fertility, but its origins and the precise significance of its rites remain unclear. After the sacrifice of a dog and goats, the blood was daubed on the foreheads of two young men, who were required by the ritual to laugh.

THE CHASE AROUND THE PALATINE
The Roman author Varro (116–27 B.C.) is the source of much of our information about the Lupercalia. Varro tells us that the Luperci, priests of this festival, ran around the Palatine Hill during the lively and raucous celebration of this festival.

THE ROMAN ORACLE

The Sibyl at Cumae in Italy was an ancient priestess, said to be the author of the Sibylline books. These were a collection of obscure verses written in Greek, which were stored in the temple of Jupiter Optimus Maximus in Rome, and consulted as an oracle during times of trouble.

The god Apollo had offered Sibyl as many years of youth as grains of sand she could hold in her hands, but when she spurned him, he allowed her to remain alive but to grow exceedingly old. When the hero Aeneas wished to enter the Underworld, the Sibyl of Cumae was his guide.

THE GREAT EARTH MOTHER

Cybele, the *Magna Mater* ("Great Mother"), was an ancient goddess who originated in Asia Minor. The cult was brought to Rome in 204 B.C. during the war against Carthage, on the advice of the Sibylline books and the oracle at Delphi. Cybele was an Earth goddess connected to fertility and nature. She was flanked by lions, and her male consort was Attis.

Cybele's followers engaged in rituals that produced ecstasy and insensitivity to pain. Cybele and Attis were worshiped during the Megalensia festival, which celebrated the rebirth of Attis and the renewal of the year. It began with a somber ceremony of mourning, which was followed by an exultant ritual called the Hilaria. The cult of Cybele may be connected to the development of Christian Gnosticism.

TEMPLE OF JUPITER VICTOR

This temple to Jupiter in his role as the protective deity of military triumph was erected by a victorious Roman general to honor the god and to beautify the city.

RITUAL BEATINGS

The priests (the Luperci), scantily dressed in loincloths made of the hide of the sacrificial goat, hit bystanders, especially women, with soft whips also made of goat hide, perhaps to induce fertility.

HOUSEHOLD GODS

The Penates (gods of the larder) and the Lares (protective deities of the household) were worshiped in private in Roman homes on three days in every month: the Kalends (the first day of the month), the Nones (the fifth or seventh day, depending on the month), and the Ides (the thirteenth or fifteenth of the month).

The Lares, according to Ovid, were the offspring of Lara, an overly talkative nymph whose tongue was cut out by Jupiter. They were often portrayed carrying drinking cups and horns.

The *paterfamilias*, the male head of the household, was charged with the care of the household gods and was responsible for maintaining the *lararium*, a shrine in the atrium of a Roman house. Worship of the household god was connected to Vesta and the hearth. A portion of each meal was thrown onto the hearth and salt and fruit were set aside on the table as offerings.

Virtuous Women

Several of the women in Roman legend represented chastity, loyalty, and obedience—virtues that the Roman state thought women should cultivate and observe. Two of these women were Lucretia and Verginia. Their stories were also related to revolution and the end of tyranny.

The rape of Lucretia

During the reign of the tyrannical King Tarquin in the late 6th century B.C., the king's sons and their kinsman Collatinus, who were in an army camp, began to argue over who possessed the most virtuous wife. They decided to ride back to Rome and go home to their wives unannounced. When they arrived, the princes' wives were all hosting decadent parties, but Lucretia, the wife of Collatinus, was still working virtuously at her wool, a traditional activity of a good wife.

Lucretia's innocence inflamed the passions of the prince Sextus Tarquinius, known as Tarquin the Proud, and a few nights later, he rode back to Lucretia's home and forced her to submit to him. When Tarquin left, she sent messages to her husband and father and made them swear an oath of vengeance. Although neither of them blamed her for what had happened, Lucretia stabbed herself with a dagger, lest any unchaste woman use her as an example in the future.

Lucretia's maltreatment and honourable death quickened the wrath of the people, who revolted against the Tarquins and founded the Roman Republic.

Freedom in death

In the 5th century B.C., a corrupt Roman official and judge named Appius Claudius lusted after a virtuous young plebeian woman named Verginia. When she refused his attentions, Appius Claudius ordered that Verginia be seized, claiming her as his slave. At the time, her

"The Death of Lucretia," as depicted in a painting by Filippino Lippi.

HORATIUS AT THE BRIDGE

During a war between Rome and Etruria, the Etruscans marched towards the one vulnerable point in the city's defenses: a wooden bridge spanning the Tiber. When the Roman army panicked, the Roman soldier Horatius Cocles ("One-Eyed") urged his comrades to dismantle the bridge while he single-handedly held off the enemy.

With just a few loyal companions, Horatius managed to stave off the invading enemy, stopping all the spears they hurled at him on his shield. Immediately he heard the bridge crash behind him, Horatius prayed to the god of the Tiber, jumped into the water in his full armor and swam across the river to safety.

Detail of a 17th-century Italian sculpture of Lucretia.

When the Etruscans attacked Rome, the besieged city grew low on supplies. A young Roman nobleman, Gaius Mucius, volunteered to steal into the enemy camp at night and kill Lars Porsenna, the Etruscan king.

However, when Mucius arrived, all the men seemed to be dressed alike. Unable to tell which one was the king, Mucius attacked the wrong man. He was seized and brought before Porsenna for questioning.

Porsenna ordered him to reveal his mission on pain of being burned alive. Mucius refused, saying that physical pain meant nothing to men seeking glory. To prove his words, he thrust his own right hand into the fire and kept it there, ignoring the great pain, until it had burned off. Admiring his courage, Porsenna released Mucius and negotiated a peace treaty with the Romans. Mucius became known as Scaevola ("Lefty").

Our knowledge of the Etruscans is enriched by bronze sculptures and artifacts that have been found in their tombs. Etruscan soldiers wore armor on the head, chest, and legs, and carried a shield and sword.

father, Verginius, was away from Rome in the army and could not come forward to prove her status—freeborn citizen or slave. But when Verginius appeared the following day, Appius refused him leave to speak and proclaimed that Verginia was a slave and his property.

Granted a few moments alone with his daughter, Verginius grabbed a knife and stabbed her through the heart, crying that only in this way would she be free. With his tale of injustice and tragedy, Verginius incited the Roman people to revolution.

Family triumph, family tragedy

In the early days of the Roman kings, Rome was at war both with Alba, the land of a nearby tribe, and Etruria. The Romans and the Albans decided to stage a battle of champions to settle the war between them once and for all. Each side sent forth a set of triplet brothers: the Horatius brothers for Rome and the Curiatus brothers for Alba.

After two of the Horatius brothers died in the fighting, the third Horatius turned and ran, not out of cowardice but as a strategy to separate his three foes. In this way he outwitted and slew all three of his opponents and, gathering up their weapons and clothes as a prize, he returned to Rome.

Horatius had a sister who was betrothed to one of the slain Curatius brothers. When she saw her brother carrying the dead man's cloak that she had made for him, she began to wail and pull her hair in traditional gestures of mourning. Horatius stabbed her in the heart, saying, "So perish all Roman women who mourn for an enemy."

Helen of Troy's Brothers

Roman mythology was very inclusive, ranging far and wide across cultures and regions, and many of the native Italic gods worshiped in Rome are quite unfamiliar to us now. This mosaic, from the 2nd century A.D., shows Romans in worship, trying to gain favor of the gods of the River Nile in Egypt.

Although Greek in origin, Castor and Pollux (Polydeuces in Greek) were widely worshiped in Rome as the *Dioscouri* ("Boys of Zeus"). Their mother was Leda and they were the twin brothers of Helen of Troy. In fact, only Pollux was the son of Zeus, or Jupiter, and was immortal. Castor's father was Leda's mortal husband Tyndareus.

Pollux, however, refused his immortality unless his brother could share in it, and so Jupiter allowed them to spend alternate days in the Underworld and in the heavens. They watched over sailors at sea and rode white horses.

The missing statues
Early on, the Dioscouri were linked with two native Italic gods, and may have been among the Penates (household gods) images that Aeneas carried with him when he fled from Troy and settled in Lavinium, in ancient Italy. According to myth, when Ascanius, son of Aeneas, founded his city at Alba Longa, he built a temple for the statues of the Dioscouri and brought them from Lavinium to Alba. The next day, they were missing from the new temple, even though the doors had remained closed.

The statues were later found resting on their old pedestals at Lavinium. Rituals and prayers were performed and the statues were moved again, but once more they vanished from the Alban temple and reappeared at Lavinium. It was finally decided that they should remain in Lavinium, and a shrine to the Dioscuri was maintained there for many years.

Lesser-known gods
Even the Romans did not know the origins of some of their gods. Consus, for whom Romulus was said to have held a festival to attract the Sabines, seems to have been associated with the storage of grain underground. He had an altar and underground granary in the Circus Maximus of Rome. These were uncovered only during the Consualia, a festival in his honor held on August 21st and December 15th.

THE JUPITER CONNECTION

Gods and goddesses were often depicted on Roman coins. A coin minted in Rome in 220 B.C. shows Jupiter driving a four-horse chariot. With him is Victory, represented as a goddess with wings, as depicted above.

The poet Ovid connected the name of Vediovis with the young Jupiter (who was also called Jove or Iove). However, most Romans regarded Vediovis as the

"opposite of Jupiter": harmful and vengeful, and linked with the Underworld. There were two temples to Vediovis in Rome and an altar at Bovillae, southeast of Rome. His festivals, during which she-goats were sacrificed, took place on January 1st, March 7th and May 21st. Outside the city of Rome, Vediovis was virtually unknown.

A LASTING ROMAN LEGACY

Mythology served a number of purposes for the Romans: it explained their origins and their ethos; it bonded together diverse peoples and religions; it demonstrated to the Romans their ultimate cultural superiority over the Greeks and other nations that they conquered.

Later, Roman mythology was important in the rediscovery of ancient literature and culture. Knowledge of ancient Greek was nearly lost during the Dark Ages and, even during the Renaissance, the most educated of scholars could usually read only Latin. The Roman versions of mythology thus exerted a powerful influence over the artistic imaginations of Renaissance painters and sculptors. That influence is still powerful today.

MOSAICS AND MURALS

The Romans loved to decorate their villas lavishly with wall paintings and colorful mosaic floors, which often featured scenes from Greek and Roman mythology.

Examples of these Roman arts can be found everywhere that the Romans built colonies, from Tunisia to Turkey. However, some of the best examples come from the cities of Pompeii and Herculaneum, south of Rome, which were both buried under mountains of volcanic ash when Mount Vesuvius erupted in 79 A.D.

A Roman mosaic of Greek mythology — Theseus and the Minotaur—from the House of the Labyrinth at Pompeii.

65

CHAPTER 5

NORTHERN EUROPE

A Viking burial site north of Alborg in Denmark. This is the largest such site in Scandinavia, with over 600 graves, each encircled by stones in the shape of a boat.

Celts and Norsemen

The Celts were the first masters of Europe. Their roots stretch well back into the 1st millennium B.C. Their culture spread in all directions from their homeland north of the Alps. By the 2nd century A.D., the Romans had driven the remaining Celts to the northwestern fringes of the Roman Empire. The Germanic tribes and the Norsemen were primarily seafaring nations. As a result, their influences spread further, reaching Iceland and as far west as North America.

The myths of Northern Europe are those of two great warrior peoples, the Celts and the Norsemen.

The Celts were the first rulers of Europe. They dominated a vast region that extended from Ireland to central Turkey, before being subjugated by the Romans. Between the 4th and 6th centuries A.D., the Roman Empire was invaded by Germanic tribes from the north and east. Around 850 A.D., their Scandinavian kinsmen—the Norsemen or Vikings—began to terrorize the coasts and waterways of Europe.

A sense of place

There are many similarities between pagan Celtic and Norse mythologies. Both tell of heroism in battle or in the pursuit of honor, and central to both is the conflict between good and evil, order and chaos, light and darkness. Both traditions include tales of giants and monsters, of voyages and quests, of divine intervention in human affairs, and of the passage of humans and gods between the real and supernatural worlds.

However, there are differences between these mythologies, reflecting the different conditions under which the two peoples lived. The Celts formed pastoral communities under hospitable conditions. Their world centered on local rivalries and disputes over land and livestock. These grew, in the telling, into supernatural adventures that take place against the real landscapes of Ireland, Wales, and Brittany.

By contrast, the livelihood of the Norsemen was always under threat from the hostile and unpredictable forces of nature. Their myths, set in a wild universe, tell of earth-shattering catastrophes, battles with frost giants, and the triumph of determination over adversity.

Making Sense of Creation

Myths can be regarded as imaginative, pre-scientific attempts to explain the mysteries of life and the universe. In myths, the forces of nature are represented as supernatural beings whose exploits are believed to be responsible for creating and governing the world of ordinary men and women.

The "all-father"

The supreme god in Irish mythology is the Dagda. He is the "good" or "skilled" god, a warrior, an artisan, a magician, and the all-powerful ruler. In Norse mythology, Odin is the "all-father." He, too, is a god of magic and of war. Both these male figures are leaders of the forces of "light" or "the sky." The Dagda heads the Tuatha da Danann, the family of the goddess Danu; Odin leads the Aesir, the gods of war, death, and power.

Earth mothers

There are many goddesses in northern mythology. The most powerful of these represent the spirit and authority of the land. By becoming the wives or mistresses of kings, they assume territorial sovereignty. In Scandinavia the main goddess is Freyja, who takes most of the gods as her lovers. Also powerful is Frigg, wife of Odin and therefore Queen of Heaven. In Irish mythology the main female deity is the triple-goddess, Medb, Macha, and the Morrigan. Welsh myths include Bran-wen, another female figure associated with sovereignty.

Sun and sky gods

Lugh is one of the few Celtic gods to have been worshiped from Ireland right across to Spain. His name means "Shining One" and he is linked in Irish

A carving on a stave church at Urnes in Norway. It depicts a deer eating leaves of the World Tree.

NORSE AND CELTIC DEITIES

Freyr Norse god of fertility and wealth. People prayed to him for prosperity and peace.

Freyja Norse goddess of love and sister of Freyr. Her necklace was made of gold by dwarf craftsmen.

Thor Norse god of Thunder with his hammer, Mjollnir.

Epona The "Great Mare" was the Celtic Goddess of horsemen and animal husbandry. Grooms made shrines to her in stables.

Loki The Norse "trickster" god. A blood brother of Odin, he was the cause of problems to befall the gods.

tradition with the Sun and light. He is a warrior, a magician, and a master of all crafts. The most prominent Norse sky god is Thor, eldest son of Odin and the giantess Jord ("Earth"). "Thor" means "thunder," and his magic hammer, Mjollnir, could produce lightning. Thor wore iron gloves to grasp the hammer, which he wielded to great effect against the frost giants. He also wore a belt that could double his already prodigious strength. Like the Dagda, Thor had an enormous appetite, and his drinking prowess could drain an ocean.

Spirits of the battlefield

The Celtic goddess of battle was the Morrigan. Taking the shape of a carrion crow or a raven, she would pick over the corpses of fallen warriors after a fray. Before a battle, the Morrigan washed the spirit corpses of warriors whose fate it was to die. There is a similarity here with Norse mythology and the Valkyries. They were the handmaidens of Odin who gathered the warriors fallen in battle whom Odin had chosen to perish, and took them to Valhalla, the Hall of the Slain. In both traditions, the gods were believed to determine the outcome of a battle in advance.

NORSE CREATION AND COSMOLOGY

Unlike the Celts, the Norsemen have left a well-developed creation myth and a detailed cosmology.

In the beginning, sparks from Muspellheim, a region of fire and light in the south, leaped across the vast chasm of Ginnungap and began to melt the ice in the frozen, northern wastes of Niflheim. Out of the ice came the frost giant, Ymir, and the cow, Audumla. The cow was attracted to the salt in the sea ice and, by licking, she uncovered the first man, Buri. His son, Borr, married Bestla, Ymir's daughter, and became the father of the warrior gods, Odin, Vili and Ve. The brothers killed Ymir and from his huge body they created the nine worlds of the Norse universe.

The Norsemen conceived the cosmos as three circular planes, like plates, suspended one above the other with spaces between. On top was Asgard, the realm of the gods and goddesses. Here they dwelt in a mighty citadel, which protected them from the rock and ice giants. In the center was Midgard—middle Earth—inhabited by human beings. Here the seas and lakes were made

of the blood of the giant Ymir. The earth was made from his flesh, the mountains from his bones, and the rocks and stones from his teeth. His skull formed the dome of the sky, supported at its four corners by dwarfs, while the perimeter wall, a defense against the giants, was made from his eyebrows. Wrapped round Midgard was the World Serpent, Jormungand, holding the tip of its tail in its mouth to maintain its grip.

On the bottom level was Niflheim, the Underworld, a cold place cloaked in perpetual night and home to the hideous goddess Hel.

Bifrost

Asgard and Midgard were connected by a fiery rainbow bridge called Bifrost. Only gods and the souls of dead warriors bound for Valhalla were allowed across. The bridge was guarded by the warrior Heimdall, armed with his trusty sword, Hofud. Heimdall would warn the gods of approaching enemies with a blast on his horn, called Gjallar.

FREYR   **ODIN**   **THOR**   **EPONA**

Heroes and Legends

The Andreas Stone, a Norse relic from the Isle of Man c. 1000 A.D., depicts scenes from the poem Ragnarok, *"Doomsday of the Gods." Here, the god Odin is eaten by the wolf Fenrir. A raven perches on Odin's shoulder.*

DIVINE LOVERS

Love is a recurrent theme in Northern mythology, often linked with jealousy and ending tragically. The love triangle in which the young wife of an old king or god falls for a younger suitor, is typical.

In the Irish story, Deirdre was destined to marry King Conchobar of Ulster but she fell in love with Naoise and forced him to run away with her. They were tricked into returning, and Naoise was put to death. In despair, Deirdre contrived her own death soon after her marriage to Conchobar.

Among the more familiar of the tragic, triangular love stories are *Tristan and Iseult* and *Sigurdr and Brynhildr*, but probably the best-known is that of Arthur, Guinevere, and Lancelot.

The earliest Celtic writing is found inscribed on stones in letters formed by straight lines to make the task easier. A variation of this script found in Ireland is called Ogham, after Ogma, the god of eloquence. Irish sagas tell of long-lost libraries of Ogham texts written on bark, of the magical properties of Ogham and of Druids (pagan Celtic priests) using it for divination, or telling the future. But the physical evidence suggests that it was used only for grave-markers and memorials.

Like the Celts, the pagan Germanic peoples did not record their ideas, beliefs and stories. However, they too had an alphabet, which also had mystical significance. Called a runic alphabet, it was believed to have been invented by Odin, and was used for incantations and carving inscriptions in wood or stone.

The accumulated wisdom of the pagan Celts and Norsemen was memorized by storytellers who passed it down by word of mouth from generation to generation. The deeds of gods and heroes were told in episodic cycles related to the calendar and to ceremonial events. The bard or poet

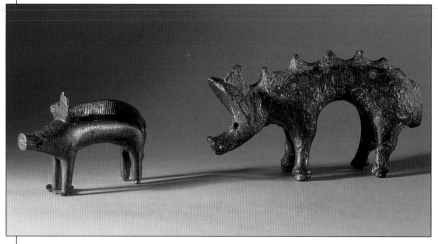

For the Celts, the boar represented war and hunting on the one hand, and hospitality and feasting on the other. The animal features prominently in Celtic mythology and in the archaeological record. These bronze boar figurines date from the 1st century B.C.

would declaim his verses or tell his stories to an audience gathered around the fire at a seasonal feast.

Celtic cycles

The earliest surviving written Celtic myths are Irish and date from the 6th century A.D. The stories follow the exploits of warriors and legendary kings in sequences, or cycles. They tell of the conception and birth of these heroes, their expeditions to the "Otherworld," their loves, their battles and, finally, their deaths.

The best-known of these myths are the *Ulster Cycle*, with its tales of the magical champion Cu Chulainn, and the *Fenian Cycle*, which tells the story of Finn MacCool, his son Ossian, and his warriors, the Fianna. The theme of a band of warrior-huntsmen, led by a mighty chief protecting his kingdom against enemy incursion, developed in Wales into the Arthurian legend, which spread through western Europe in the Middle Ages.

Norse sagas

It was in the far north that interest in the old gods lasted longest. Around 1220, Snorri Sturluson, an Icelander, compiled an anthology of stories about the heathen gods called the *Prose Edda*. Its authenticity is partly confirmed by comparison with events celebrated in the *Poetic Edda*, a collection of loosely related poems thought to be much earlier in origin.

Another major source is Skaldic verse, the compositions of court poets, or *skalds*, beginning in the 9th century and continuing through the Viking era into the Middle Ages.

VOYAGES AND QUESTS

Typical of the "Imram," Irish tales of voyages to the Otherworld, is that of *Bran, Son of Febal*. Bran's goal was the Land of Women, where there is no grieving, winter or want. After an eventful journey, he returned home to find that his family and friends were long dead, and that his voyage was remembered by their forebears as ancient history. Another such story involves Mael Duin, who set off to avenge his father's death and found himself trapped for a while in the Land of Women.

Examples of quests also abound in medieval Welsh and European literature. To win the beautiful Olwen, Culhwch accepted a challenge to find 39 objects for her father, the giant Ysbaddaden; while Owain, inspired by Cynon, son of Clydno, went in search of the Castle of the Fountain. In the most famous quest of all, the knights of Arthur's Round Table pursued the elusive Holy Grail. In fact, this story developed from a much earlier Celtic legend of a quest to retrieve a magic cauldron.

HUNTING AND FISHING

Celtic and Norse mythology both feature hunting and fishing. One of the longest hunts takes place in the Welsh story of *Culhwch and Olwen*, in which Arthur and his men race over Ireland and Wales in pursuit of the boar, Twrch Trwyth, before running it into the River Severn.

In the *Fenian Cycle*, Finn MacCool, as a youth, burned his thumb on the Salmon of Knowledge while he was cooking it for his master, Finneces. Thereafter he had only to bite his thumb to know the future.

In Norse mythology, Thor went fishing for the Midgard Serpent with the giant Hymir, using the head of Hymir's ox as bait. After a fearsome struggle with the monster, Thor hauled it to the surface and would have killed it with his hammer if Hymir had not cut the fishing line. Had Thor succeeded, Midgard, which was held together by the serpent's coils, would have been destroyed.

An illumination from an early Icelandic manuscript showing King Harold Fine-Hair cutting the fetters from the giant Dofri, who was to become his foster father in folklore.

Custom and Ritual

A Norse picture stone c. 750 A.D. shows the god Odin on his six-legged horse, and a burial ship.

To the Celts, fire symbolized the Sun, and they marked the annual cycle of its seasons with four great bonfire festivals. The main ceremonies heralded winter and summer and were called Samain and Beltaine, respectively. The other two, Imbolc and Lugnasad, took place in February and August. The Scandinavians had equivalent celebrations. The most important of these, as with the Celts, was held at the beginning of winter and went on for days. It was known as The Winter Nights.

Blood sacrifice

Classical commentators have reported fertility rites and human sacrifice associated with Celtic festivals, particularly with Samain. Victims were drowned in vats in honor of the god Teutates or burned in wooden cages to propitiate Taranis. Priests called Druids, who possessed considerable power and influence, presided over these rituals.

The Norse, too, are reported to have indulged in human sacrifice at the great temple of Uppsala, in Sweden. The Scandinavians had no priesthood order, and it was usually the king or chieftain who made contact with the gods on behalf of the people at sacrificial feasts.

More archaeological evidence exists for animal sacrifice than for human, and for offerings in the form of valuable items such as weaponry and jewelry. Other offerings, in the form of foodstuffs, were brought by ordinary people to groves, rocks, and boulders in which local gods were thought to live. Ceremonies were conducted over an altar made of piles of stones.

FUNERAL SHIPS
The wealthiest Vikings were buried in ships that were crammed full of their belongings, including livestock and even servants, which, it was believed, would be needed in the next world. The ships were then buried under mounds of earth or set alight and turned into blazing funeral pyres. For the same reason, the Celts also buried a deceased person's valued possessions, such as wine and joints of pork, with them. A Celtic warrior might be transported to his grave in his chariot, and this would be buried with him, perhaps to carry him onward to the Otherworld.

FIGUREHEAD
Viking ships had prows and tips of sterns carved with human or animal figures. Typically, the prow would be in the form of a snake's head and the stern a curled snake's tail.

AMULETS
Scandinavians wore amulets, or charms, in their clothing, inscribed with runes to protect them from disease and sorcery. The symbolic power of Thor's hammer, Mjollnir, was well-known.

FUNERAL MOUNDS

Two of the most famous Viking ship burial mounds were unearthed at Sutton Hoo near Woodbridge in England and at Oseberg near the Oslo Fjord in Norway. At Sutton Hoo, buried along with the 28 meter-long ship were sledges, beds, kitchen utensils, and weaving equipment. The Oseberg ship, 21.5 meters long, contained 15 pairs of oars, an anchor, and a bailing bucket.

FUNERAL PYRES

While the Celts celebrated bonfire festivals, their literature shows little evidence of the practice of human fire sacrifice. However, the Greeks and Romans describe foul rituals presided over by the Druids, including the burning alive of victims in huge wicker images of men.

THE OTHERWORLD

Odin lived in the silver-roofed hall of Valaskjalf. He sat on a throne, called Hildskjalf, from which he could survey the nine worlds of the Norse cosmos. He decided the fate of warriors in battle, ensuring that his favorites died and joined his personal band in Valhalla. Here, every night, they feasted on pork and quaffed endless supplies of mead milked from the goat, Heidrun. The following day, they ventured forth to die again in battle.

The Irish Otherworld hostels, or Bruidhen, resembled Valhalla, with feasting, music, and lovemaking. Another Irish image of the Otherworld, Tir na Nog, or the Land of Eternal Youth, was also an idyllic place. It was here that Oissin followed his lover, Niamh, and stayed happily for 300 years.

In Wales the Otherworld was called Annwn and it features in the story of Pwll. The hero offended Arawn, Lord of Annwn, and exchanged places with him for a year to make amends. Apart from having to kill Arawn's enemy, Pwll did not find the Otherworld an unpleasant place. It had a darker side, though, in the 10th-century poem *The Spoils of Annwn*, claiming the lives of most of Arthur's men who were in pursuit of a magic cauldron.

THE END OF THE WORLD

In Norse mythology the event is called Ragnarok. It will be foreshadowed by civil war, Midgard will be gripped by the Winter of Winters, the stars will fall and the earth will crumble. Monsters of the underworld will break free and the World Serpent will rise from the encircling ocean and flood the Earth.

Then there will be a ferocious battle between the gods and the frost giants in which all will be killed except Surt, the fire demon. He will ignite the remains of the world, destroying humankind and consuming the fallen warriors. As the flames reach up to the heavens, everything will sink into the sea.

But this will not be the end. When all is destroyed, the Earth will rise again from beneath the waters, fair and green. The sons and daughters of the gods will replace their forebears and from the shelter of the tree Yggdrasill will emerge a human couple, Lifthrasir and Lif, to repopulate the Earth.

Gods and Spirits in Everyday Life

T he Celts believed that their gods and goddesses had powers to heal and protect, and to influence the outcome of ordinary, everyday events. When they asked a favor of a particular deity, they would also make an offering. If they were appealing to a water goddess, such as Sulis, they might throw some of their most valued possessions into a well or lake. As late as 1868, there was still a Celtic-style festival held in Cevennes in France in which valuables and livestock were offered to the gods by casting them into a lake.

Life and death

The Celts and Norsemen had no conception of heaven or hell as a reward or punishment for the lives they led. The Vikings may have preferred a hero's place in Valhalla to a place in the Underworld, but they believed, nonetheless, that rebirth into the afterlife was automatic. Indeed, one writer tells us that, so firm was the Celts' belief in the afterlife that they would even put off paying debts until they met up again there! This may account for the heroic way they threw themselves into battle, with no apparent fear of death.

Sacred places

The Celtic belief in the presence of spirits in all natural things gave rise to open-air worship. Groves were particularly favored because of the sanctity of individual trees, particularly the oak. Classical writers refer to such sacred groves in Marseilles, Anglesey, and Drunemeton in Asia Minor.

Celtic deities were linked with specific natural features. Springs, for example, were thought to be the homes of goddesses in the service of the Earth Mother, the source of all life. A case in point is Sulis, who guarded the hot springs at Bath in the west of England. Lakes and pools were sacred as entrances to the Otherworld. Other such gateways to the supernatural kingdom include the *sidhe—*

A panel from the Gundestrup cauldron, from the 1st century B.C. Surviving examples of Celtic cauldrons are richly decorated with sacred imagery, and this one from Denmark is the most magnificent of them all. It depicts the nature god, Cernunnos, sitting cross-legged among the animals. Cauldrons had a spiritual place in Celtic homes and society, and a magic cauldron features in the original Arthurian legend.

A carving from the 12th-century Hylestad stave church in Norway showing a scene from the story of Sigurd. Regin the Smith reforges the broken sword.

LEGACIES

Many echoes of pagan Celtic and Norse cultures may still be found in customs such as kissing under the mistletoe at Christmas or holding bonfire parties in the fall. Pagan festivals have been absorbed into the Christian calendar: for example, Samain is now "All Saints' Day" or "All Hallows' Day" (hence, "All Hallows' Eve" or "Hallowe'en").

In English, four days of the week are named after northern gods. Tuesday is Tyr's day; Wednesday is Odin's or Woden's day; Thursday is Thor's day, and Friday is Frigg's day.

The names of gods persists, too, in place-names across Europe; the cities of London and Lyons, for example, are named after Lugh. Also from Lugh, we get the "leprechaun," a diminutive latter-day parody of a once proud god.

The most widely recognized legacy of Celtic mythology is the Arthurian legend, which is as potent today as it was in the courtly Middle Ages. The story has been retold countless times in various forms, from novels and feature films to musicals and Disney cartoons. The wise old figure of Merlin can be seen both in Gandalf, a creation of the novelist Tolkien, as well as in Obi-Wan Kenobi in the film *Star Wars*.

Similarly, the Norse pantheon and stories continue to inspire great art, such as Wagner's *The Ring Cycle* operas and the popular fantasies of Tolkien. Irreverent but no less sincere in its homage to the Norse vision of the universe is Terry Pratchett's *Discworld*.

The struggle between Christianity and paganism, as shown on a 12th-century tapestry from Skog Church, Sweden. The three figures to the right are ringing bells to frighten away evil spirits and pagan gods.

ancient Irish burial mounds—where the gods were thought to dwell in comfort.

Norse settlers chose striking natural features as holy places, such as the rocky hill of Helgafell ("Holy Mountain") on the southern shore of Breidafjord in western Iceland. Sometimes it was the gods who did the choosing, as in the story of Thorolf Mostrarskegg. As his ship approached Iceland, Thorolf threw the wooden pillars of his high seat overboard and followed where they drifted until they reached land. There he built his home. Ever after, the site was deemed holy because it was thought to have been chosen by Thor.

Both the Celts and the Norsemen also had permanent sanctuaries for communicating with the gods. The best-known of these was the magnificent temple in Uppsala, which was razed to the ground in the 12th century. It contained huge statues of Thor, Odin, and Freyr.

CHAPTER 6

CENTRAL AND EASTERN EUROPE

*The lakes and forests of Finland—
a typical view of "Moist Mother Earth."*

Beyond the Vistula

T he mythology of Central and Eastern Europe belongs to the Balts, Slavs, and Finno-Ugric peoples. The classical writers of the first and second centuries A.D. called the Balts and Slavs the "Vanedi"—"the people living beyond the Vistula river." Today they are known as the peoples of northeastern Europe who speak Indo-European languages such as Lithuanian, Slovene, Slovak, and Russian.

The languages of the Finno-Ugric peoples belong to a different group, the Uralic family, which spread from the direction of the Ural mountains, in Russia. The Finno-Ugricians, which include the Finns and the Lapps, were widely influenced by their Indo-European neighbors and their myths and legends are similar.

Moist Mother Earth

The character of Central and East European mythology reflects the living conditions of the people. Much of the land that they colonized was covered by vast, dense forests and divided by rivers and great lakes. The damp, marshy terrain was represented in folk tales as *Mati-Syra-Zemlya*— "Moist Mother Earth."

Life was fraught with danger for the forest-dwellers, who lived in fear of wolves and bears. But, equally, people who dwelt on the exposed expanses of the treeless steppe were prey to marauding nomads and the Mongol-Tartars.

Slavonic-speaking peoples emerged as a distinct group from the varied, mobile mass of people living in the Balkans and in Central and Eastern Europe. Slavonic tribes dispersed from the region of the Carpathians to form the countries that we recognize today.

The battle for survival

People survived by fishing and hunting, by farming and by grazing cattle in forest clearings and meadows. They depended on the elements for their livelihood and on the forest for shelter. Powerless to control the forces of nature, they sought to identify and understand them by personifying them as numerous gods. In this way stories, myths and legends evolved about the Sun and the cosmos, the Moon, the wind and thunder and lightning, and about the spirits of the forest, the river, the crops, the stable, and the household.

DUAL FAITH

Christianity began to spread through these regions around 1000 A.D., but it was only in the cities that the new religion took a hold. Throughout the Middle Ages in remote, rural areas ancient beliefs survived beneath a thin veneer of Christian ritual. In medieval Russia, as late as the 15th century, religion could be described as a "dual faith." Indeed, vestiges of pagan belief are found in stories, folklore, customs, poetry, and biographical writings well into the 19th century.

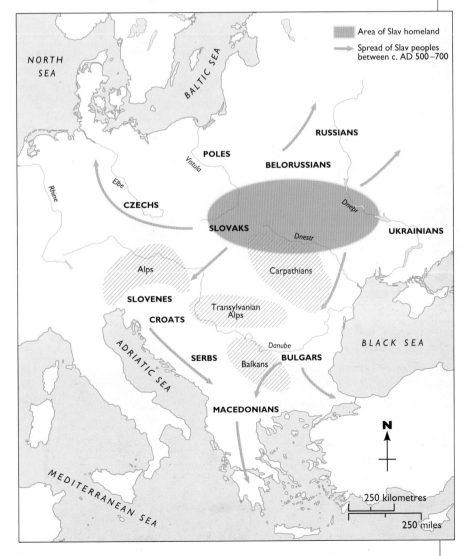

Area of Slav homeland

Spread of Slav peoples between c. AD 500–700

Gods, Spirits, and Forces of Nature

Slavic myth evolved gradually through three distinct overlapping stages. First, came the belief that the world was governed by the creative power of light and the destructive forces of darkness. Hence the well-being of humankind depended on people's ability to enlist the support of good in the struggle against evil.

Next came the belief that every household was protected by the spirits of dead ancestors, who determined the health and fertility of the living. Allied to this belief was the cycle of the seasons, death, and rebirth, and rituals involving contact with the souls of the dead in the Otherworld.

Concern with fertility also related to the cults of the chief Slavic god, Svantovit, and the mother and daughter deities, the Rozhanitsy.

The third stage was the emergence of gods that personified the Sun, the Moon, the Earth, the sky, fire, thunder, war, trade, fertility, and much besides. Some myths about the Sun and the Moon portrayed them as lovers, marrying at the beginning of summer and parting in winter. Their offspring were the stars, and their quarrels were earthquakes.

Ancient Slavonic dieties

The father of all the Slavonic gods was Svarog, the sky god, known to the Balts as Svantovit. He was the father of Dazhbog (the Sun) and Svarozhich (fire). These were the most important elemental gods: they provided light and warmth in a land that was cold for much of the year. The god of thunder and lightning was Perun.

In her earliest form, Baba Yaga was the Great Goddess of Slavonic myth and patron of women. With the coming of Christianity, she was transformed into the grotesque handmaiden of the Devil. She was said to live in a revolving house deep in the forest and to feed on children. She was also supposed to travel in a large, iron mortar using the pestle as a paddle, as in this French magazine illustration from 1904.

His thunderbolts were a potent fertility symbol because they were thought to awaken the Earth in spring. Perun was also the god of war, who rode across the sky in an iron chariot pulled by an enormous goat. He had a battle-ax which, when he threw it, would always return to his hand.

Mokosh was a truly ancient Slavic fertility goddess who is closely associated with Moist Mother Earth. She is often represented in the company of the bird-dog, Simorg.

The beginning of the world

In Finnish mythology, Luonnotar, the Daughter of Nature, was lonely and unfulfilled. She dived into the sea and was made fertile by the foam. But, having no place to rest where she could bear children, she continued to float, in torment, for seven centuries. Eventually a teal, looking for somewhere to nest, settled on Luonnotar's knee, which projected from the water. The duck built its nest and laid seven eggs.

When Luonnotar moved, the eggs rolled into the sea and down into the abyss. There they were transformed into the stuff of the universe. Their bases formed the earth, and their upper parts the heavens. Their yolks became the Sun, and their whites the Moon. The spots on the shells became the stars. Other fragments formed the clouds. Finally, Luonnotar fashioned the shoreline, the ocean bed and the mountains to support the sky. Now she had somewhere to rest and have children.

THE OLD MAN AND THE SALT MILL

Vainamoinen was the god of song and poetry and the greatest hero of the Finno-Ugric myths. He was already old when he was born and is often portrayed as an old man playing a stringed instrument called a kantele. Following his miraculous birth, Vainamoinen cleared the Earth and sowed it.

On his mother's advice, Vainamoinen sought a wife in the land of Pohjola. His journey there was disastrous. He lost his horse in an ambush and found himself swimming for his life for eight days in a stormy sea. Eventually, an eagle scooped him up and carried him to the Pohjola border where, lost and disheartened, the old man dissolved in tears. His sobs were heard by the young and beautiful daughter of Louhi, the Lady of Pohjola. Louhi promised Vainamoinen her daughter's hand in marriage if he would forge for her the Sampo, a talisman consisting of a flour mill, a salt mill, and a money mill.

Returning home, Vainamoinen asked his brother, Ilmarinen, the divine smith, to make the Sampo. Ilmarinen agreed, delivered the talisman in person to Louhi and claimed her daughter's hand for himself. The Sampo changed

Pohjola from a barren, snowy wasteland into a land of plenty. Years later, Vainamoinen and Ilmarinen tried to steal it from Louhi. In the resulting struggle, the Sampo fell into the sea where it was destroyed except for the salt mill, which continues to grind out salt on the ocean floor.

Millponds were said to be haunted by the Vodyanoi, chief of the water demons, who was visualized as a huge fish covered with moss. He was said to destroy dams and mills.

Russian mythology tells of the Domovye, or household spirits. Here is grandfather Domovoi, shown as a gray-bearded old man with his body covered in hair. Tradition had it that if the family moved house, the Domovye had to be taken with them or they would torment the new owners.

Appeasing the Spirits

THE TREE OF LIFE

The Tree of Life, according to the Slavs, contained the seeds of every living plant. So sacred was this tree that it was guarded by a dragon, Simorg, a creature that was part dog, part bird. Unfortunately, the tree looked like any other tree and Simorg was invisible. This made the work of the woodcutter very dangerous because he might fell the Tree of Life unwittingly. Before cutting down any tree, an elaborate ritual had to be performed to appease the invisible dragon that might be guarding the tree and to ensure that it was not the sacred tree.

W ell into the 20th century many Slavs, even if they were Christians, still believed in a host of minor household and other divinities. To pacify these various spirits, they maintained certain customs and practiced set rituals.

Household gods and nature spirits

The main spirit of the house was the Domovoi. Superstition prevented people from even mentioning his name and so he was referred to as "grandfather" or "himself." His voice or sobs and groans were often heard but people went to great lengths not to see him. He was thought to be humanlike in appearance, but with silky fur, horns, and a tail.

Other domestic gods were the Dvorovoi, the spirit of the yard, the Bannik, the spirit of the bathhouse, and the Ovinnik, the spirit of the barn. Household spirits were held to be generally friendly. It was customary to treat them with respect, however, to gain their help. To please the Dvorovoi, people would leave a little sheep's wool, a glittering object or bread in the stable.

Among the more fearsome spirits were the shadowless Leshy and the mischievous Polevik. They were, respectively, the spirits of the forest and the fields, who revelled in leading travelers astray. An offering of two eggs and an elderly cockerel, placed in a secluded ditch, would, it was believed, placate the Polevik.

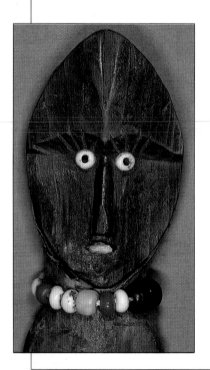

The wooden head of a traditional sacred hunter, adorned with a bead necklace. This modern shamanistic symbol is used by the Selkup people of Siberia.

SHAMAN RITUALS

All Finno-Ugric peoples practiced an animistic religion centered on the supreme power of the shaman. The word "shaman" (feminine "shamanka") means "one who is excited or raised up." It relates to the trancelike states that these magicians fell into when their spirits were believed to be wandering in the Otherworld.

Sometimes their spiritual journeys were compared to climbing a ladder or tree; sometimes they were described as flying like a bird or on the back of a winged horse.

FIRE AND FIREDOGS

Rural Slavonic people with strong shamanistic beliefs held fire in such awe that parents forbade their children to shout or swear when the household fire was being lit. "Firedogs"— the metal gates used to hold logs in an open fire—originate from the shaman association of fire with spirits and gods.

RECORDING THE MYTHS

The first written Slavonic sources date back to the 9th and 10th centuries A.D. and the conversion to Christianity. Among them were the "wonder tales" —*volshebnye skazki*—which were written down in the 9th century but are much earlier in origin.

These old epic poems relate the exploits of the Russian *bogatyrs*: heroes who had magical powers that they used to protect their homeland. In later accounts, the *bogatyrs* became champions and heroes of the Christian cause.

The chief source of Finnish myth is the *Kalevala*, a long, continuous epic poem compiled from folk songs in the early 19th century by the Finnish scholar, Elias Lonnrot. It tells the story of the struggle between Kalevala, the "Fatherland of Heroes," and the "back country," or northern regions. The poem includes the Creation myth and the deeds of heroes, such as Vainamoinen, and ends with a look to the future and the coming of mortal kings.

SACRED FIRE
Fire has always been sacred to Slavs. In many Slavonic countries it is still treated with a mystic respect among rural communities. Fire was a divine gift that was brought to the Earth in the form of lightning bolts cast by Svarog, the sky god. Traces of this ancient myth can be found in stories of fire-breathing serpents such as the twelve-headed Goryshche that was vanquished by the Christian hero Dobrynya Nikitich.

BELLS AND NOISE
As the shaman danced round the fire, small bells attached to his clothing rang incessantly, to ward off evil spirits.

WATER SPIRITS
Millponds were supposedly inhabited by the Vodyanye— water spirits that were said to destroy dams and mills to let the water run freely. To win the goodwill of the Vodyanye, it was not unknown for millers to push passers-by into the mill-race to satisfy the gods' appetite for flesh.

Rusalki were water spirits that were the souls of drowned maidens. People in different regions had their own ideas of what they were like. In the north, they were imagined as naked, pale and demonic, while the southern Rusalski were more attractive and wore light robes of mist. But both enticed men to their deaths with promises of love. The northern Rusalki did it for fun. The southern Rusalki, however, truly loved their victims and it was considered a blessing to drown in their arms. To avoid the attentions of the Rusalki, people carried a leaf of absinth.

WARDING OFF SPIRITS
The shaman was thought to have the power to send his spirit forth in any form to commune with other spirits or to defend himself and others against evil influences. Leather tassels attached to clothing or shields were believed to help disperse the spirits.

DRUMMING
Beating of the magic drum, conjurations and incantations were all intended to exert power over people, animals, plants, trees, stones, water, the weather, and the seasons.

Sacred Objects and Enduring Images

WEREWOLVES

The ancient belief in werewolves, people who change into wolves at night, was particularly prevalent in late medieval Europe. The revival of the myth at that time was possibly due to stories of Vseslav, an 11th-century pagan prince from Belarus who fought so fiercely that he was said to become an animal.

People born with prominent birthmarks, tufts of hair on the body, or an afterbirth caul were thought likely to be werewolves. In some places this was seen as a sign of good luck because such children were supposedly gifted with second sight. It was also supposed that they could choose to turn into different animals or fish, and that only those who were malevolent opted to become bloodthirsty wolves. Werewolves were said to be invulnerable to all but silver weapons.

The pre-Christian gods of Central and Eastern Europe were not sought in temples or through the medium of a priest. Svantovit had a temple and priests at Arcona, on a Baltic island, but this was unusual. More often, rituals and ceremonies were conducted under an open sky with a prince or military leader presiding.

In 980 A.D. the Russian prince Vladimir I marked the beginning of his reign by erecting a group of idols on a hill next to his palace. These included a wooden Perun with a silver head and a golden moustache as well as the figures of the deities Khors, Dazhbog, Stribog, Simargl, and Mokosh. After he was baptized, however, Vladimir had them cast into the Dnepr river. Thereafter, as Christianity spread, large sculptures of pagan gods disappeared.

Paganism in folk art

Magic symbols and images of the pagan gods have survived in amulets and jewelry found by archeologists as well as in Slavonic folk art. The icon corner was not only the focal point of a Russian house but the visible testament to an enduring dual religious heritage. Here Christian icons draped with towels stood alongside household objects decorated with traditional, pagan imagery.

The sacred tree, sacrificial altars, goddesses, animals such as horses and snow leopards, and Perun's axe were all common decorative devices in folk art. Sacred imagery also included abstract motifs based on natural forms with magical powers. For example, sky deities were suggested by a zigzag, representing lightning, a disk, for the Sun, and a swastika for fire.

A scene from the movie Werewolf of London, *made in 1935. In many werewolf stories, the person changes himself back into human form by taking a special potion. The term "werewolf" comes from the Old English "werwulf," meaning "man-wolf."*

A wide-ranging legacy

The myths of Central and Eastern Europe are still very much alive, not only in traditional customs and sayings but in the more sophisticated, industrial urban culture of the region.

Even today, in the Ukraine people still invoke the wrath of Chernobog in the curse, "May the black god destroy you." When Russian carmakers were looking for a name for their new range, they called it Lada, after the Slavonic goddess of beauty and fertility. Songs about Lada and her male counterpart, Lado, are still often sung by women planting grain and at weddings.

In 1914, Sergei Diaghilev, founder of the Russian Ballet, invited the artist Natalya Goncharova to design sets for *The Firebird*, a ballet with music by Igor Stravinsky that was based on a Russian folk tale. Such collaborations, which sought to combine contemporary esthetic ideas with inspiration from native Russian folk art, have had a profound effect on modern performing arts.

A scene from Goncharova's The Firebird.

VAMPIRES

The word "vampire" means "undead." It refers to a corpse, usually of a pagan or sinner, that becomes animated at night and has to suck the blood of the living to survive. Although widespread in Central and Eastern Europe, vampire lore had its greatest hold among the western and southern Slavs.

The origin of the vampire myth is obscure, but can be traced to the Black Sea area where, in ancient times, people believed that spirits could be conjured from the underworld by pouring warm blood on the ground.

Many ways of disposing of vampires were devised, some intended to help the wretched creatures to rest in peace, others to destroy them. One of the latter was to drive a sharpened hawthorn or aspen stake through the body.

A modern interest in vampires was stimulated by Bram Stoker's novel, *Dracula*, published in 1897. Stoker added new aspects to the myth including the idea that vampires were shape-shifters able to change into bats or wolves. Parts of his story were based on the exploits of Vlad the Impaler, a fierce 14th-century Transylvanian warlord.

This house in Romania has the Tree of Life carved round the doorway to ward off evil spirits.

CHAPTER 7

AFRICA

A rock painting depicts antelopes and giraffes grazing together, in Nswatugi Cave, Zimbabwe. Animals play an important part in African mythology.

From the Sahara to the Veldt

Africa is a patchwork of tribes and cultures where more than 1,000 languages are spoken. Its peoples fall into three broad ethnic and cultural groups that roughly correspond to Africa's North, Central, and Southern geographic divisions.

In the Sahara Desert and arid lands of the North, people are often nomadic, migrating with herds of sheep, goats, and camels. Over thousands of years they have mixed with Europeans and Arabs and, as a result, their culture has been influenced by Islam and Christianity.

The tropical rainforest and bush lands of Central Africa are home to the continent's original inhabitants, such as the Bushmen and the Pygmies, whose cultures still survive. This region provides a rich source of African mythology.

In the savannah and veldt grasslands of Southern Africa, black Africans live alongside people of European and Asian descent, who brought with them their own cultures, traditions and mythologies. Here European culture has had a wide influence.

An artistic record

In Africa the traditions are oral: writing was never developed. Africans have always loved telling stories but only in the 20th century were these stories collected and recorded, mostly by Europeans and Americans.

The traditional African way of keeping cultural records was through art. Some of the earliest surviving examples of African art are the 1,000-year-old rock paintings of the Sahara and East and South Africa, depicting wild animals, cattle, hunters, and religious figures. Oldest of all are the terracotta heads of the Nok culture of northern Nigeria, which date back at least 2,000 years.

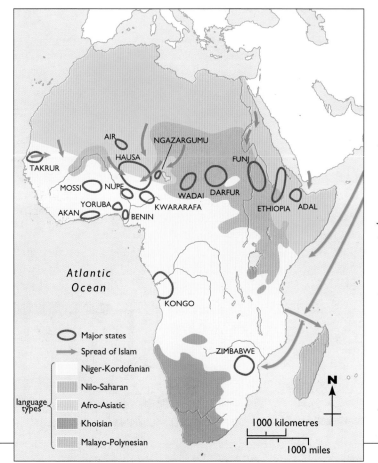

During the 1st millennium A.D., towns and states developed across western and central Africa and in the south. This was the result of the growth in trade between peoples from Mediterranean North Africa and south of the Sahara, and between southern Africa and Asia. It resulted in a mix of cultures and mythology, with the emergence of several distinct groups of peoples across most of the continent.

The Great Creator and Protector

A 17th-century brass plaque from the palace of the Benin Oba people, West Africa, shows a family sacrificing a cow, the most prestigious animal sacrifice.

A bronze head made by the lost-wax process of casting. This is thought to be a portrait of an Ife king, Oni, from the 13th century, but it is sometimes identified with the West African sea god Olukun.

The peoples of Africa were highly religious long before Arab traders or European missionaries arrived to spread Islam and Christianity among them. Traditional African beliefs usually included a "High God," who was often a sky god associated with thunder and lightning. This God was also the creator God, who was regarded as a bountiful father to humanity, and the God of grace to whom prayers were offered. These beliefs are still very much alive today in Africa, even among African Christians and Muslims.

Idia, the mother of the Benin King Oba Esigie, was granted the right to establish her own palace and ancestral altars as a reward for using her mystic powers to bring victory in Benin's war against the Igala tribe. Brass heads with the long-beaded coral cap that covers the queen mother's hairstyle were cast for these altars in the 16th century.

Worship of the elements

In African religion, the elements Sun, Moon, and Oceans were gods. The Earth god was usually female, and the Sky male. One of the best-known Earth goddesses is Ala of the Ibo people in West Africa. She is ruler of humanity, the source of morality, and protector of the harvest. She is also the giver of fertility to humans. As queen of the underworld she receives into her womb the departed, and must grant permission before a grave is dug. Shrines to Ala are found all over Ibo country and sometimes special festival houses are built in her honor.

THE TALE OF THUNDER AND LIGHTNING

In myth, the animals of the forest often became magical characters in their own right, sometimes personifying the elements of nature, as in the story of Thunder and Lightning.

Long ago Thunder and Lightning lived on Earth in the form of a sheep and her son, a powerful ram. He regularly used to lose his temper and cause devastation among the people, burning their houses and fields, and his mother would chastise him in a voice like thunder. Eventually people got together and exiled him to the forest. Even there he continued to wreak havoc, starting terrible forest fires, while his growling mother still chastised him. At last everyone had had enough and the two were banished altogether, sent far away up into the distant sky, from where the ram could do no harm. But from time to time he still loses his temper and sends down to earth bolts of fire—Lightning—accompanied by the loud rumbling cries of his mother—Thunder.

The story of race

A Yoruba myth tells how God protected the first humans, who lived in the ancient, sacred city of Ife, which is today in Nigeria. The Yoruba believe that Ife is the center of the world; that from here humans spread out across the planet. Their myth calls to mind the biblical story of Babel.

Originally, they say, all humans spoke one language, were of one color and were equal in every way. They had all they needed and were in direct communication with God. But they became bored and complained to God, asking Him to make them different from each other. God warned them that this would lead to strife but they took no heed. So He agreed to their request and, inevitably, there followed feuding. Thus the human population was divided into different tribes and races, each with their own language, and they were scattered around the world.

UNDERWATER SECRETS

Many myths describe spirit worlds that exist alongside the visible world. These may offer rewards but their secrets are to be feared. The Alur people living beside Lake Albert tell of a young fisherman who used to fish in the deep waters of the lake.

One day the fisherman noticed the water was glistening. He scooped some water into his boat and, before his eyes, it turned into shining pearls. Looking into the water, he saw beautiful, creamy-colored goats gliding beneath the surface. Mesmerized, he jumped overboard and sank to the bottom. He found it rich with emerald-green grasses grazed by goats. A figure of unearthly beauty, the Lake God, embraced him and made him his goatherd.

The fisherman stayed there and herded the white goats on the bottom of the lake and forgot his earthly life. Years went by, until one day he remembered his wife and children. He told the Lake God he wanted to go home.

"You are free to go," said the Lake God, "but never tell anyone what you have seen. If you do you will die at once."

The fisherman rose to the surface and found his boat full of pearls. He returned to his family but he was a changed man, given to silence. He sold the pearls and bought white cows, which he spent his time herding. One day with some friends he drank too much.

"I have been to the bottom of the lake," he said aloud. "I have herded the Lake God's goats and drunk their milk. . ."

Before he could say more he was dead.

87

Hunting and Other Perils

Hunting is the oldest occupation in Africa, and one of which many Africans have some experience. Even among tribes who are settled as cultivators, hunting remains an important source of food. But hunting will always be risky because of the hidden dangers of the forest.

The courage of the hunter has been highly prized, and honor was bestowed on successful hunters. Some of these were revered as heroes possessed of magical powers. Taboos and rituals, such as dancing or painting the body or rubbing it with magic oil, were used to help make the hunt more successful. Without these performances, people believed, the quarry would hide and be invisible.

A staff used by devotees of Shango, the Yoruba spirit of thunder and lightning, during dances in which they are possessed by the gods.

A Yoruba wooden sculpture depicting a female spiritual figure. It is 90 cm high and is decorated with paint and pigments.

ANIMAL FRIENDS, ANIMAL VICTIMS
Some myths tell of the closeness of the world of humans to the animal world. They describe friendships between people and animals, often attributing to animals human characteristics. A solemn occasion shared by humans and animals is when an animal must be sacrificed to please a god or to keep good relations with the family's ancestors. In some cultures this is a regular event. The blood of the victim, it is believed, contains its life force, which in turn will nourish the deity.

A group of East African warriors perform a raindance. Rainmaking is an important magical function. There are magicians who specialize in this art, or tribal festivals may be arranged with special dances for this purpose. Rainmaking has also become a part of conventional religion in Africa, where Christian or Islamic hymns supplicate the Almighty to send rain.

Dangers of the forest

Other dangers awaited the hunter in the forest besides wild animals. A story from the Mali tribe tells of evil men who developed a taste for human flesh. They had the power to change into hyenas at night and would terrorize the human settlements, dragging off their victims to the jungle to eat them. The villagers believed that these hyena men really existed and they were particularly afraid at night.

The forest was the source of life but it was also a place to be feared. It became the abode of forest spirits who could be evil and treacherous. These spirits are believed to exist all around humans, though often unseen.

A typical Yoruba story describes the dangers of disturbing the spirits of the bush. It tells how a farmer decided to clear land in the forest to sow corn. The elders of his village advised him against disturbing the spirits of the bush but he was stubborn.

Against their advice, he proceeded to clear the bush, but was soon surrounded by mischievous spirits. At first they seemed to be helping him, and he made progress, but he was unable to control them and they eventually wrought havoc for him and his family, destroying his crops and attacking his wife and children. In some versions of the story they kill him; in others they simply chase him away. This story typifies the ambiguity of the bush spirits. They can be asked for help, but if they are crossed they can do enormous harm.

THE HUNTER WHO COULD CHANGE SHAPE

To lure animals into being caught, or to protect themselves, some hunters knew how to change into animal shapes. In a story from Nigeria, one hunter became so successful at this and killed so many animals that the animals decided they must do something to stop him.

One of the elephants knew how to change into a man, and, in disguise, entered the village and shared palm wine with the hunter. While the two of them were drinking, the hunter boasted of his magic secrets: how he could turn into many different forms, one after another, to avoid being harmed. Just as he was about to give away his final secret, his wife stopped him.

The next day the elephant charged the hunter in the bush. As the hunter changed forms, the elephant recognized each one and attacked it. At last the hunter resorted to his final secret: he turned into a fly. This form was unknown to the elephant who had to admit it had lost the contest. Thus the hunter escaped, but never told anyone his secrets again.

Magic, Healing, and the Old Culture

Much of the traditional religion and mythology of Africa has been lost or overlaid during 500 years of contact with Europe. But it is still possible to see temples and shrines, like the reconstruction here of the Yoruba temple of Shango, god of storms, at Ibadan, Nigeria. One of the most attractive parts of Africa for the early European explorers and traders were the coastal regions of West Africa, such as modern-day Ghana, Benin, and Nigeria, which had great wealth.

Today, old traditions persist mainly in tropical Africa, where the best-known surviving groupings are the Ashanti in Ghana and the Yoruba in Nigeria. These two are also the main source of most of the recorded African mythology.

In Southern Africa the dominant religion is now Christianity, and in the North it is Islam. Nevertheless, underlying more recent influences are the values and myths of traditional Africa, which have so much power to shape the hopes and fears of Africans in the modern world.

FEARING THE WORST

During European expansion in Africa, many stories circulated among Africans about the perils of dealing with these powerful but uncivilized strangers. It was said that their arrival had been foretold in dreams of yellow or red people who came out of the sea with iron rods that spat fire, and who lived in houses built on platforms pulled by oxen.

An altar made from wood and stone in a small Dogon settlement in Mali, West Africa.

People in Africa still believe in the power of magic, especially to heal the sick. All illnesses are attributed to psychic or magical causes and are often traced to the influence of someone who envies or hates the victim, and may have looked upon that person with an "evil eye."

Traditional medicines use mixtures of herbs to produce a magical effect in patients, or charms and amulets to protect them from harmful influences. Most villages have at least one medicine man or medicine woman, commonly called *Nganga* in South and Central Africa, who is usually the first person to be consulted in times of illness. Only later, if this does not work, will people resort to western medicines if available.

RAM CARVING
Animals feature in African mythology and in religious rites. Bronze and wooden carvings, like this ram's head, are often used to represent ancestors. A figure of a lion, the king of the jungle, is used to symbolize authority, power and strength. The hare is depicted as an animal trickster.

FABLES OF AFRICA

Animal fables have always been popular in Africa, and from there they have spread all over the world. The Brer Rabbit stories were brought to North America by black African slaves. Some of Rudyard Kipling's *Just So Stories* also originated in Africa. Such tales explain why things are the way they are, or illustrate moral lessons. Typical characters are the lazy Tortoise, the crafty Hare, the wise Elephant and, as in this story, the resourceful Frog.

In ancient times a king had two sons, Frog and Lizard, and had to decide which of them should inherit his kingdom. They were away traveling, so he sent word that the one that would reach his court first would be the next king. The two princes both set off at once. Lizard was faster, and was soon far ahead. Meanwhile Frog thought of a plan. He knew Lizard hated rain, so he sprinkled rainmaking powder and soon rain was falling in torrents. Frog was happy and hopped along. Meanwhile Lizard, who was still far ahead, waited under a rock for the rain to pass. But the rain lasted for a long time and Frog arrived first at court. His heralds blew their trumpets and the king announced that he would be the one to inherit the kingdom. When Lizard finally arrived he was greeted by Frog:

"You may have beautiful skin, brother Lizard, and I may be ugly, but I have won and I will be king."

Ever since then, when people hear the frogs croaking, they say, "Listen to Prince Frog's heralds blowing their trumpets. Soon it will begin to rain."

DECORATION
Wooden pillars, carvings, and figures are often painted to represent animal coloration or gods or spirits of diseases such as smallpox. Red, white, and black are important colors. Red is associated with royalty, white with spiritual power, and black with ordinary people.

PRIESTS
The head of the family or clan usually acts as priest when sacrifices are made, and looks after the shrine.

THUNDER AND LIGHTNING
The Yoruba believe that Shango became god of thunder, lightning, and rain after hanging himself on a tree and ascending to heaven. Thunder is believed to be Shango's bellowing.

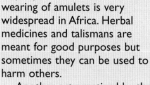

DOUBLE-HEADED AX
Among the Yoruba, the double-headed ax is a common symbol. It represents Shango, the storm god, who is said to throw his ax, the thunderbolt, when there is a storm.

THE MEDICINE MAN
The role of Nganga is of great importance, requiring a special kind of person who, at an early age, is called to his or her vocation. Sometimes the young man or woman will undergo ritual initiations before learning the secrets of the herbal potions that they will later administer. It is also the Nganga who gives amulets or specially-made charms to people to ward off evil. The wearing of amulets is very widespread in Africa. Herbal medicines and talismans are meant for good purposes but sometimes they can be used to harm others.

Another art practised by the Nganga is divination, a kind of clairvoyance. The Nganga will advise on future misfortunes, such as famine, sickness, or war, and how to avoid them. Diviners consulting spirits or departed ancestors usually go into a trance, sometimes needing special interpreters to translate their utterances. Others make predictions using astrology, the patterns made by objects thrown on the ground or the movements of birds.

Chapter 8

INDIA

A 16th-century Indian book illustration showing a battle between Arjuna and the Kurus, watched by Brahma and the gods in the sky.

Indian Prehistory

The peoples of ancient India did not think it important to record their history. They lived simply and cremated their dead in a climate that quickly eroded anything manmade. They left little behind in the way of historical records, ruins, or burial grounds, the usual yardsticks for measuring ancient history. But what they did leave—to their eternal glory—was a rich literature.

The Sanskrit hymns called the Vedas date back to at least 1500 B.C., and are our main source for understanding the early culture of India. They contain the beginnings of the myths that later shaped Indian civilization. The earliest hymns are the 1,000 or so gathered in the Rig Veda: poems of ten verses or more each describing a mythical world of gods and goddesses who personify the forces of Nature, such as Agni, god of fire, and Usha, goddess of the dawn. Within these hymns lies what many believe to be a secret wisdom that was later to evolve into the spiritual teachings of the Upanishads and the Vedanta, and the foundation of classical Hinduism.

Aryan invasion

The myths of the Vedic hymns show the influence of the early peoples of Iran and central Asia, the most easterly group of the Indo-Europeans. These people, who called themselves "Aryans," entered the subcontinent of India between 3000 and 1500 B.C. How much they contributed to the development of the Vedas or to what extent Vedic wisdom was already present in India is unclear.

The Aryans found in India at least two indigenous cultures. The Indus Valley culture of northern India flourished between about 3500 and 1700 B.C. At about the same time, the Deccan Neolithic culture blossomed in southern India. India's culture and mythology combine all these different strains.

The cities of Mohenjo Daro and Harappa in present-day Pakistan show evidence of the ancient mix of cultures of Aryans and indigenous Indus Valley peoples. These settlements, with their paved streets, meticulous sanitation, and carved script, as yet undeciphered, show evidence of an advanced civilization. From here, early Hindu beliefs spread throughout India. Later, around 500 B.C., Buddhism evolved near present-day Nepal and Bengal, then spread south and east. India's mythology is a mix of Hindu and Buddhist beliefs.

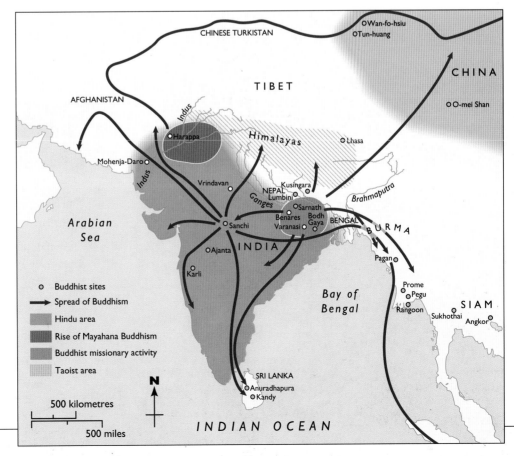

The Gods of Nature

The Vedic universe is filled with the great spirits called Devas. Each of them embodies an aspect of nature, such as Agni, the god of fire, Vayu, god of the wind, and Varuna, god of the ocean. The two great deities to emerge from the early myths are Vishnu and Shiva, who became known as the gods of Maintenance and Dissolution respectively. Both have their ardent devotees who honor them as the Supreme Deity, and their separate traditions of learning and worship.

A wood and glass figure of Garuda, mythical carrier of Lord Vishnu, from Tamil Nadu, south India.

Vishnu the Preserver
Vishnu is the background to existence who gives birth to Brahma the creator, and then enters the universe as Narayana, the "one who lies on the Waters of Life." He sleeps at the base of the universe, attended by the goddess Lakshmi. Whenever there is disturbance in the balance of the universe, Vishnu takes on mortal form to restore the true religious teachings and protect righteousness.

He is represented as full of mercy and patience. His symbols are the lotus flower and the conch shell, by which he blesses the good, and the club and discus, with which he subdues the bad. His role as just and dutiful ruler is seen in his embodiment as Rama, whose story is told in the *Ramayana*. Vishnu takes on the role of teacher in his incarnation as Krishna, who appears in the epic *Mahabharata*.

Shiva the Dissolver
Shiva reveals the dark side of the divinity, the power of death and destruction. He is easily moved to anger—a frightening figure, surrounded by ghosts and goblins.

A Hindu bathes in the waters of the Ganges. All great rivers in India are worshiped as female deities such as Ganga and Narmada.

But Shiva is easily pleased and is merciful to his devotees, showing special favor to the *asuras* (the "ungodly"), and to those who are at odds with the world.

Riding on the bull Nandi, he carries a small drum to accompany his dance of destruction. On his head are a crescent moon and a symbol of the descending waters of the River Ganges, which he caught in his hair to save the mountains from being crushed under its waters. His home is Mount Kailash in the Himalayas, where he has numerous followers. He is also found in cremation grounds, where he smears his body with ashes and sits in a trance of meditation.

Ganga, the river goddess

The goddess Ganga is the spirit of the River Ganges and daughter of the Himalayas. She was taken up to heaven as the celestial Milky Way and brought back to Earth by the penances of King Bhagiratha, to be caught in Shiva's hair. Her devotees believe that she washes away sins. This mystical story accompanies the physical existence of the river in a union of myth and reality that typifies the world of Indian myth, where the dividing line between the visionary and the material is subtle and shifting.

A 10th-century A.D. bronze figure of Nataraja–Shiva as the lord of the dance. He is shown as a four-armed figure encircled by flames. Among his disciples today are the ascetics who wander India, semi-naked, smeared in ashes and smoking ganja (marijuana).

REINCARNATION

A thread that runs through all Indian myth is the everlasting play between the worlds of illusion and reality: on the one hand the perpetual cycle of birth and death, of creation and destruction, of the duality of good and bad; on the other, the divine existence of the immortal soul and the Supreme Truth. This tension is present in the drama of reincarnation, in the periodic descent of the avatars (bodily forms) of Vishnu from the eternal to the temporary worlds, and in the tireless human search for *mukti*—liberation from the world of birth and death.

Vedic wisdom teaches that each living being in this world is an eternal soul inhabiting a temporary body. The individual soul, called the *atma*, is a particle of the Supreme Truth. By its presence as the self, the soul gives energy to the body and to the universe. Each soul has its own desires to enjoy the world, and to fulfil these desires it enters the cycle of rebirth, called *samsara*. When the soul leaves the body at death, it is born into another body, like an actor changing clothes. Moving from body to body in search of happiness, the soul passes through all forms of life, from insect to god, until it finally achieves liberation and is reunited with the Supreme Truth.

Families at War

Krishna with his childhood sweetheart, Radha. Her all-consuming love for him symbolizes the love of the soul for God, and is celebrated in Hindu art and poetry.

The epic *Mahabharata* is the story of the struggle for the throne of India, written down at least 2,000 years ago and relating events from a much earlier period in Indian history. It centers on the rivalry between two groups of brothers: the five sons of King Pandu, called the Pandavas, and the 100 sons of his brother Dhritarashtra, called the Kauravas.

Pandu died young and his brother Dhritarashtra was made regent. Pandu's young orphaned sons were trained to be brilliant warriors and statesmen, fit to rule the kingdom. But Dhritarashtra wanted his own sons to inherit the kingdom and a feud arose between the two groups of princes. The rivalry gave way to hatred when the Kauravas plotted to burn the Pandavas alive in a palace of flammable lac specially built for the purpose. The Pandavas escaped but, after being cheated

THE "SONG OF GOD"

Krishna spoke the immortal words of Bhagavad Gita, or "Song of God," in a dialogue with his friend Arjuna, at the dramatic climax of the *Mahabharata*.

The teaching begins with the *atma*, or the self. Krishna describes the self as an immortal soul, which is reincarnated from one body to another. The soul, he says, cannot find satisfaction in the temporary pleasures of this world, because it is eternal. He advises that the soul should work without attachment to the results of its actions, to victory or defeat, but simply for the sake of doing its duty. He teaches that all living beings are the eternal children of God and will find happiness if they surrender their every action in devotion to God. This will free the self from the cycle of birth and death and allow it to return to the eternal spiritual realm to be reunited with God.

In a modern miniature painting from India, Jatayu, lord of the vultures, tells Rama where he can find his kidnapped wife, Sita. Rama was the god Vishnu in human form, and the story of his life is told in the epic Ramayana.

Bas-relief on the 12th-century temple at Angkor Wat, Cambodia, showing the bloody battle between the Pandavas and the Kauravas.

in a gambling game, were forced into exile for twelve years. They swore vengeance.

Death and reconciliation
Krishna befriended the Pandavas and used his influence to try to bring about a peaceful solution to the dispute. But, in the end, nothing could prevent all-out war. All the royal houses of India were drawn into the conflict, pitting brothers, relatives and friends against each other in mortal combat.

At the moment the battle was about to begin, the Pandava hero, Arjuna, lost his nerve and turned to Krishna for help, whereupon Krishna delivered his immortal teaching, the Bhagavad Gita, in which he revealed his identity as God Himself.

The battle raged for eighteen days. Millions died, including the 100 sons of Dhritarashtra. The Pandava brothers were almost the only ones to survive. Disillusioned, they lived on to rule their kingdom, having lost all their friends. At the end of their lives, they left for the Himalayas to prepare for death. In paradise they were reunited with their cousins, their enmity over, and the whole drama was revealed as the illusory play of the material world, in which nothing is as it seems.

RAMA'S JOURNEY OF THE SOUL
The *Ramayana*, the "Journey of Rama," tells of Rama's banishment from his kingdom and his battle with the forces of evil to rescue the goddess Sita. The divine Rama's human journey provides an allegory for the journey every soul must make, in which it endures banishment and loss, faces its own demons, and eventually finds redemption.

The *Ramayana* is often performed in the towns and villages of India and throughout Southeast Asia. People believe that to hear or witness Rama's struggles is to relive their own lives in a divine context. The story of the Ramayana is interpreted by some as an allegory for the meeting of the Aryan and Dravidian cultures in south India. The civilizing Aryans, represented by Rama and the kingdom of Ayodhya, encounter the indigenous Dravidians, represented by Ravana and the kingdom of Lanka. But the themes of the *Ramayana* go much deeper, to the release of the soul from the age-old struggle between good and evil.

CREATION MYTHS

In one version of the creation story, the universe grew from one of the countless seeds emanating from the body of Vishnu, floating in the Ocean of Creation like clusters of bubbles. Each seed became a golden egg, into which Vishnu entered as the Purusha, the Cosmic Person. His mouth became Speech, His nostrils became Smell, His eyes became Sight, His legs became Movement, His veins became rivers, and His heart became Mind.

Another account attributes the creation of the universe to the god Brahma, who was born from the navel of Vishnu. Brahma made the planets and stars and all the thousands of demigods, each of whom was given charge of a particular part of the cosmic order. However, powerful as the demigods are, behind them lies Vishnu, and it is He who creates and controls all. Without Him they can do nothing.

Social and Religious Orders

SACRED ANIMALS
Animals have a special place in Indian culture. This is because of the belief in reincarnation, which places the same soul in both animal and human, only in different incarnations in the cycle of rebirth. One of the most famous mythical animals is the monkey-god Hanuman, an incarnation of the Wind God and a devoted servant of Rama. All over India roadside shrines are dedicated to Hanuman.

SPECIAL CREATURES
The cow is revered as a mother and must never be harmed. All things to do with the cow, including her dung, are pure. The ghee, or clarified butter, made from her milk is universally used for cooking and as fuel for lamps and sacred fires in the temples.

The peacock is a native of the woodlands of northern India and a favorite symbol of beauty and grace. The cry of the peacock foretells the arrival of the monsoon rains. The peacock feather is the symbol of Krishna, who always wore one in his hair.

The elephant is often kept by temples to lead their religious processions as the bearer of the temple deities. The heavenly elephant Airavata is the bearer of Indra, Lord of Heaven. To harm an elephant brings great misfortune; to feed one brings blessings.

A sadhu, *or holy man, in Pushkar, Rajasthan. He and his fellow* sadhus *are an ever-present reminder of the virtues of simplicity and renunciation.*

Traditional Vedic society was divided into four Varnas, or social groups, which gave it great stability and longevity. These groups were compared to the four parts of the body —head, arms, stomach, and legs.

The Brahmins, or priests and teachers, were the head of the social body, giving intelligence and direction; the Kshatriyas, the ruling class, were the arms, providing administration and protection; the Vaishyas, or farmers and businessmen, were the stomach, giving nourishment; and the Sudras, or workers, were the legs, supplying skills and labor.

Just as in a healthy human body, where all four parts would work harmoniously, so, in theory, the four social orders would work together for the benefit of the whole. To some extent, this happened in practice. Vedic society was fair and just— for example, they never had slavery and everyone had access to the rule of law—

but, under the caste system, privilege thrived and people were forced by birth to live disadvantaged lives. Those without caste, such as the tribal "outcastes," were often denied basic rights. Nowadays, social reforms have relaxed or even completely abolished the strict caste system, although it still dominates rural areas and tends to dictate marriage partners in Hindu society.

Guru and disciple
The spiritual teachings of the Vedic scriptures have been kept alive by the system of guru, or teacher, and disciple. Hindu society divides the passage of life into four stages, progressing from student to final renunciation. Eventually, the Sannyasi— someone in the final stage—may become the guru of the rest of the society, teaching by example the importance of giving up all attachments to material life in preparation for leaving this world at the time of death.

Sadhus
Many Sannyasis travel the length and breadth of India with barely any possessions, depending entirely on others'

Two cows rest in a street in Old Dehli crowded with pedestrians and cyclists. In Indian cities, a cow's gentle nature makes her an ever-present reminder of the virtue of patience on the streets.

THE FOUR ORDERS OF THE HINDU RELIGIOUS FAITH

In Hindu teachings, all actions produce effects in the future. This is the law of *karma*. Hindus who perform their religious duties faithfully and behave honestly and properly in ordinary life will be rewarded with a desirable rebirth, or reincarnation. The following are the four passages of life.

Brahmacharya
(Student life). Age 10–25. During this period the student lives with his guru, or teacher, as a celibate monk, learning the scriptures and being trained in renunciation.

Grihastha
(Married life as a householder). Age 25–50. The householder is expected to enjoy life in a moderate way and give support to the other three religious orders.

Vanaprastha
(Retired life). Age 50 plus. The husband and wife, having raised a family, retire from worldly life and devote themselves to the good of the community and to spiritual practices such as going on a pilgrimage.

Sannyasa
(Complete renunciation). Any age. Not everyone reaches this fourth order, but those who do are accorded great respect. The Sannyasi lives a solitary life of complete celibacy and simplicity, traveling from place to place to teach and to practice austerity.

generosity for their daily needs. These holy men, and sometimes women, are called *sadhus*. They practice detachment from the world the better to devote themselves to spiritual realization, following the advice of Krishna in the Bhagavad Gita:

Happiness and distress appear and disappear like the passing of winter and summer. They arise from the perception of the senses and you must learn to tolerate them without being disturbed.
(Bhagavad Gita 2:14)

The renunciation of the *sadhus* sets an example, making them objects of veneration. Even today a genuine *sadhu* ranks higher than anyone in Hindu society. An advanced *sadhu* may become a guru and accept disciples who live with their teacher in the ashram, or place of spiritual shelter, following a daily routine that begins before dawn with bathing, worship, and study of the scriptures.

Krishnattam dancers perform in brilliant make-up and costume, relating stories from Vedic myths. In India, music and drama are central to religion, myth, and philosophy.

Temple Communities and Townships

Adoration of the Ganges—a celebration around the temple and along the river banks and bridge at Hardwar, an important piligrimage site in northern India.

For thousands of years a temple has stood at Srirangam, on the sandy island formed by the confluence of the sacred River Kauveri and River Kollidam, in the southern Indian state of Tamil Nadu. It is typical of ancient Hindu temples throughout India.

The temple is dedicated to a deity of Vishnu named Ranganath, who lies on His right side, one arm extended towards the worshiper, His eyes closed in Yoga Nidra—the trance-sleep of Vishnu in which He dreams the universe into being. Vishnu is the God of Mercy and Grace, to whom most Hindus pray every day.

Temple communities

Over time the temple at Srirangam has grown into an entire township. Seven concentric walls surround it, each pierced by four gateways, called Gopurams. A different community is to be found within each successive wall—pilgrims to the temple, temple artisans, merchants, cooks, priests, scholars, and, in the innermost compound, the monastic quarters and the temple school where future priests and scholars are trained.

TEMPLE COMPLEX

Bhubaneswar in northeast India is a city of temples; at one time, there were more than 1,000. Several temples are built around a large reservoir which is believed to receive water from all the holy rivers of India. It is used for ritual bathing, so that pilgrims and residents alike can purify themselves.

One of the most impressive temples at Bhubaneswar reservoir is Lingajara. It was built in 1014 A.D. to the glory of Shiva. The temple has a central dancing hall and an audience or offerings hall, a sanctuary, and a communual area. Throughout the day, Hindus visit the temple to make offerings, pray, sing, and listen to teachings.

DANCING HALL

Dance dramas telling the history of the Hindu religion, through which worshipers revere Vishnu and Shiva as the Supreme Deity, are held in the central dance hall.

HALL AND REFECTORY

At the front of the temple are the communal areas where pilgrims gather before visiting the shrine, to be fed on sanctifed vegetarian food from the temple kitchens.

HINDU FESTIVALS

Festivals are a vital part of Hindu life. They are so numerous that hardly a day goes by without one being celebrated somewhere in India. The festivals follow the Hindu calendar, which is based on lunar months, beginning from the month of Caitra (March/April).

Ramnavami (April)
> The birthday of Rama.

Vaisakhi (April/May)
> The first day of the month of Vaisakha, the beginning of the New Solar Year. For some Hindus, this is their New Year's Day. On this day, Hindus bathe in holy water.

Raksha Bandhan (July)
> As a token of dedication between brothers and sisters, the sister will tie a thread around her brother's wrists.

Janmashtami (August)
> The birthday of Krishna, when the image of child Krishna is bathed. Celebrations last until midnight, the time of his birth.

Dassehra (October)
> Celebrations for victory of Rama over Ravana. Giant effigies of Ravana are burned amid fireworks and pageantry.

Navaratri (October)
> Nine nights of dancing and festivities in honor of the goddess Durga.

Diwali (October/November)
> Lamps are lit at night and placed in windows and doorways to welcome Rama back to Ayodhya after rescuing Sita. Diwali marks the Hindu New Year and is a time for closing business accounts.

Shivaratri (February/March)
> The birthday of Shiva.

Holi (March/April)
> Spring festival commemorating the play of Krishna, when he and his friends sprayed colored dyes on one another. It is an occasion for carnival and merriment. Holi also celebrates the rescue of the devotee Prahlada from fire by the demoness Holika.

SANCTUARY TOWER
A 45-meter-high tower with colorful figures of deities, mythical beasts such as nymphs, and amorous couples, rises above the walls.

AUDIENCE HALL
Here worshipers can attend elaborate ceremonies and listen to teachers expounding and retelling the sacred myths of Hinduism.

SANCTUARY
Here lies the shrine to Shiva. In some temples there is a separate shrine to the female consort of the main deity—Parvati or Durga for Shiva and Lakshmi for Vishnu. The figure of Nandi the bull is usually found alongside shrines to Shiva. The bull is an ancient and important symbol in Hindu culture.

RELIGION IN THE HOME
As well as worshiping in temples, most Hindus have shrines in their own homes. There, the family can offer daily prayers, sanctify food, and honor their gods. The home itself is thus transformed into a small temple, where the daily cycle of life can be lived in harmony with the Divine, according to the teachings of Krishna in the Bhagavad Gita:

> Whatever you do, whatever you eat, whatever you offer and give away, and whatever austerities you perform—do these as an offering unto Me. In this way you will be freed from bondage to work and its auspicious and inauspicious results. With your mind fixed on Me in this principle of renunciation, you will be liberated and come to Me. (Bhagavad Gita 9:26–28)

Pilgrimage in Modern India

Pilgrims bathe in Lake Pushkar, near Jaipur. Pushkar is India's major temple dedicated to Brahma.

Modern India is a land where tradition and modernity are cheek by jowl. The latest Japanese cars, manufactured under licence in India, compete for road-space with cows and buffalo carts. A burgeoning middle class with access to the latest consumer goods lives in a modern democracy but shares an ancient culture. Indian society is changing fast but, especially outside the cities, it is still dominated by religious traditions such as the pilgrimage.

For many Indians, pilgrimage is still a major occupation. Millions of people regularly visit the great Tirthas, or holy places, across the subcontinent. A major reason for pilgrimage is to create good fortune, countering the inauspicious effects of poor horoscopes or family misfortunes. Another reason is to earn merit in the eyes of God so as to be assured of a good future birth, or even of release from the cycle of rebirth. In modern India, life

is still very hard for most people, and problems such as ill-health, poverty, and unemployment, exacerbated by the pressure of growing population that has now passed one billion, are all too common.

Honoring the Lord Krishna

A popular place of pilgrimage is Vrindavan, Krishna's birthplace, just south of New Delhi, on the road to Agra. Vrindavan lies at the heart of Vraj, the once-forested region where Lord Krishna lived. The whole region has been worshiped for thousands of years, and was the setting for many of the events recorded in the *Mahabharata*, the epic history of ancient India.

Many pilgrims to Vrindavan begin their visit by rolling in the sand, because Krishna walked on this sand and made it sacred. They might also wear markings on their foreheads made of yellow clay from the local soil, to gain Krishna's protection. On their first day, pilgrims will bathe in the sacred River Yamuna, where Krishna

During the festival of Navaratri, fireworks explode around an effigy of the demon-king Ravana from the Hindu epic of the triumph of Rama over evil.

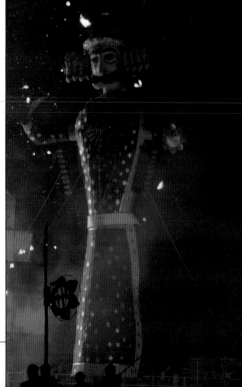

bathed, to purify themselves of their karma—all that they have brought with them from their previous lives.

Vrindavan is a town of 5,000 temples. Very early in the morning, two hours before sunrise, they come to life with their morning ceremonies, to awaken Krishna for the new day. They bathe the image of Krishna, dress Him, and feed Him. While this goes on, bells ring out and visitors arrive, announcing their presence by calling out the names of Krishna and his consort Radha.

Circumambulating a sacred place

One of the important parts of any pilgrimage is the Parikrama. Every sacred Hindu place has a Parikrama path—a pilgrim route encircling the site.

The performance of Parikrama, or walking round a holy place, is one of the most potent ways of showing one's respects. Clockwise, the walk represents the process of living centered on the particular deity that resides at that sacred place; of realizing one's true potential for self-motivation and self-direction while yielding to the pull of the inner divine source of being. The circle is the expression of the movement and the stillness: the balance between dynamic motion and the calm center. It represents the equilibrium of the inner and the outer life.

A Hindu woman, wearing the traditional sari, prays at a temple in Varanasi. Throughout India there are thousands of pilgrimage sites, from sacred mountains to rivers, temples, and small shrines.

BOLLYWOOD AND THE NEW MYTHOLOGY

Nothing reveals the contrast between old and new so much as the Indian film industry, known as "Bollywood," the East's answer to Hollywood, USA.

On the one hand, Bollywood is the purveyor of an affluent Western lifestyle that is quite beyond the reach of most cinemagoers in India and its actors are national heroes. On the other, it continues to make religious films and TV "soaps," such as the long-running *Ramayana* and *Mahabharata*, which celebrate the mythology and spirituality of traditional Hinduism.

The influence of television is dramatically undermining traditional beliefs among the younger generations. Whereas once the pictures displayed in every three-wheeler taxi would be of the driver's favorite deities, nowadays, in younger drivers' cabs, they are often of Bollywood film stars, who are busy creating for India a new mythology.

CASTE AND GENDER
A great challenge to modern India is social reform to give equal opportunity to all. It is still the case that those from low-caste origins and women are denied many basic rights. Legislation has been introduced to redress this imbalance, but in practice, outside the more affluent classes in the big cities, attitudes are slow to change.

CHAPTER 9

CHINA AND SOUTH-EAST ASIA

A small shrine, the Temple of Happiness and Longevity, stands on the shore of a lake in Xinjiang province in China.

The Ancient Origins

The early myths of the vast land now called China—home to one-fifth of the planet's peoples—and its neighbors in East Asia, are lost in the mists of time. The myths that have descended to us today built upon those earlier myths. They were collected in the 2nd century B.C., in the reign of the first Chinese emperor, Ch'in Shih Huang Ti. Huang wanted to impose a cultural unity on his vast empire, and was prepared to modify or destroy any records that did not serve his purpose.

The first religion
At least 10,000 years ago shamanism, which could be regarded as the world's first religion, spread into Mongolia and China. The shaman was someone who went into a trance to communicate with the animal world and the spirit world, and was believed to assume the shape of animals. Shamans developed systems of divination, using animal bones and shells to foretell the future. Some fragments of early myths dating from the 9th century B.C. and showing shamanic influences have survived.

Early Chinese myths
Two principal figures from early mythology were the divine brother and sister, Fu Hsi and Nu Kua. They were half-human and half-animal—with human heads and serpent bodies—which shows their shamanic origins. Nu Kua formed humans from the yellow Earth, lifted the sky into place over the Earth and, with Fu Hsi, created human progeny and all aspects of civilization. Later came the legendary Yellow Emperor, the bringer of order, who is said to have ruled around 2500 B.C. He is revered as the one who introduced divine knowledge into human society, especially arts of medicine.

Chinese mythology is a mix of influences from shamanism, Buddhism, Taoism, and Confucianism. Shamans were powerful in ancient China, then Buddhists arrived from India around 400 B.C. Confucius lived in China around 500 B.C. but his philosophy and teachings gained power only after his death, at a time when warring states and imperialism caused instability. Taoism emerged in China around 100 B.C. Various mountains in China are regarded as sacred and are visited by pilgrims.

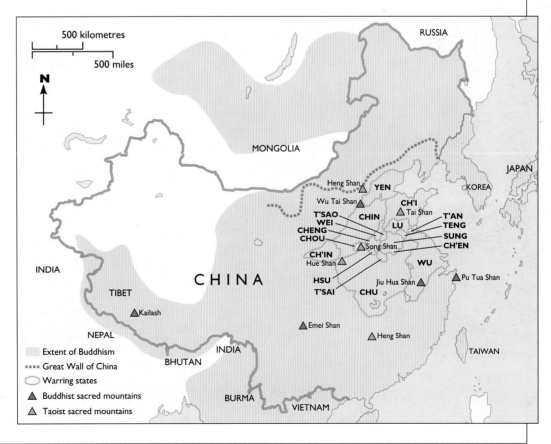

The Undefined Religion

The Tao gives birth to the One.
The One gives birth to the Two.
The Two give birth to the Three.
The Three give birth to the Ten
    Thousand.

LAO TZU'S LAST JOURNEY
Lao Tzu despaired of the world and left the royal court. Travelling west he eventually came to the edge of the kingdom, reaching the mountain pass called Han-Ku. Here he spent the night with the gatekeeper.
  The gatekeeper realized that Lao Tzu was leaving for ever, and begged him to write down his profound thoughts to leave behind for the benefit of all. Lao Tzu agreed, and the result was the *Tao Te Ching*, the great book of Taoist wisdom. He then passed through the gate and was never seen again.

The heart of the very earliest Chinese vision of the cosmos is the Tao, the origin of all that is. The Tao cannot be defined, because it exists beyond all forms. In the words of the great Taoist sage, Lao Tzu:

The Tao that is spoken of is not the eternal nature of the Tao. That which can be named is not the true Tao.

The process by which the Tao gave rise to reality is defined in Lao Tzu's great classic *Tao-Te Ching* as follows:

These words describe how the Tao, the essence of all, gives birth to Nature—the One—which in turn gives birth to Yin and Yang—the Two. Yin is female: moist, cold, the Moon, fall and winter, shadows, and waters. Yang is male: dry, hot, the Sun, spring, and summer, brightness and earth. From the perpetual striving of Yin and Yang arises the Three—Heaven, Earth, and Humanity. Humanity must try to balance the opposites of Heaven and Earth.

At the end of this cosmic progression comes the appearance of all living beings —in Chinese tradition referred to as the Ten Thousand. However, going backward, as the great sage Chuang Tzu advised, we find that within each living

A 17th-century Chinese painting shows fathers explaining to their children the meaning of the traditional black and white Yin-Yang symbol. Taoists believe that the two forces are in everything, locked into an eternal struggle in which neither can destroy the other.

LEGEND OF THE *I CHING*
The *I Ching* oracles are based on the patterns made by 64 hexagrams. One legend tells us how the mythical figure Fu Hsi, who ruled all below heaven, discovered the eight Trigrams that form the basis of the 64 hexagrams upon the shell of a sacred turtle, which emerged from the sea as he stood on the shore.

being are contained the Three, the Two, and the One. In the Tao all are linked, interconnected in a fundamental unity of existence. It is the search for this inward unity that preoccupies the followers of the Tao.

Taoism and paradox

Because all life is a struggle between the opposites of Yin and Yang, in which first one then the other appears to have the upper hand, all life is full of surprises and paradoxes. This is the Tao.

The Way of the Tao teaches that nothing can be defined; all forms are changing and temporary, as illustrated in this story:

The great sage Chuang Tzu once dreamt of being a butterfly. He flitted happily from tree to tree and forgot he was Chuang Tzu. Then he woke up and found himself as the same old sage. But he wasn't sure who he was: was he the butterfly dreaming he was the man or the man dreaming he was the butterfly?

THE EIGHT IMMORTAL HEROES

The Eight Immortals are popular semi-divine super-heroes in China, even to this day. They are worshiped and honored, and their help is invoked by Chinese all over the world. The eight represent a cross-section of the different levels of Chinese society:

Lu Tung Pin is associated with medicine and healing, and gives those who worship him charms to protect them from ill-fortune.
Ti Kuai Li was forced to live in the body of a deformed cripple, although he previously was a handsome man. He especially helps the weak and oppressed.
Chang Kuo Lau accidentally ate some magic herbs and thus became immortal. He rides a donkey backward and favors couples seeking children.
Ts'ao Kuo Chiu was a murderer who repented and became immortal.

Han Hsiang Tzu is usually depicted on the mountains, listening to the music of nature. He carries a flute.
Han Chung Li carries a peach that gives immortality to the eater.
Lan Ts'ai Ho is a transvestite who sometimes appears as a woman.
Ho Hsien Ku was a young woman who was made immortal because of her generosity and asceticism.

Figures of the Immortals made out of joss and painted. Burning joss is an offering for a lifetime of good karma.

At Lung-Shan temple, Taipei, in Taiwan, a village elder tends candles lit in honor of his ancestors. Chinese mythology holds that the dead watch over their living relatives.

Emperors and Immortality

THE CRUEL EMPEROR AND THE WOMAN IN THE MOON

A story told at the time of the Mid-Fall Festival of the full Moon explains how a young woman achieved immortality and now lives on the Moon.

There was once an emperor who was cruel and hated by his people. He wanted to live for ever and ordered a search for the pill of immortality. The pill was found and brought to him and he announced that he would consume it, much to everyone's dismay. To prevent this from happening, his young queen stole the pill from his bedside and swallowed it herself. As soon as she did so, she floated up to the Moon. There was great rejoicing among the people. To this day, when the Moon shines brightly she can be seen smiling down and is honored as the one who saved the people from their cruel emperor.

The Forbidden City, in modern-day Beijing, was completed in 1421. It proclaimed the Emperor's divine status as representative of Heaven on Earth.

Part of the Chinese mythological world is tied up with the quest for immortality. People believed that it was most desirable to prolong one's life in the physical body for as long as possible, if not for ever. This idea gave rise to a mythology of immortality, for example the Eight Immortals. It also resulted in the building of great tombs for Chinese emperors and leaders.

When the first emperor, Ch'in Shih Huang Ti, died in 210 B.C., his might was demonstrated in the huge underground monument created for his burial. Its construction lasted throughout his reign, and all the artisans who worked on it were put to death and buried with him. Part of the monument includes a life-size terracotta army buried to guard him in his next life.

In their attempts to make the human body imperishable, people took doses of materials that seemed to last for ever, such as gold or mercury. The result, of course, was that many died from metal poisoning. Other substances were concocted from herbs and animal products, such as mushrooms or the vital parts of long-lived animals like tortoises and bats.

A HAN DYNASTY BURIAL

The Han dynasty lasted from 206 B.C. to 200 A.D. A remarkable find from the early part of this period is the tomb of Lady Xin, the wife of the prime minister of the kingdom of Changsha, which encompassed most of present-day Hunan province. The tomb is filled with a vast array of everyday items, figurines, provisions, and clothes to accompany Lady Xin's body into the next life.

MOUND BURIAL AND PRESERVATION

The wooden burial vault is about 9 meters underground and is covered by an earth mound 4 meters high. The mound contains the graves of Lady Xin's husband and son.

The vault is embedded in a mix of charcoal and clay, which has preserved Lady Xin's body in almost perfect condition. An autopsy showed she probably died of a heart attack.

SERVANTS FOR THE AFTERLIFE

At the head and feet of the body lay 162 wooden tomb figures. These are models of female attendants, musicians and dancers. Each is 50 centimeters high. There are also taller figures representing manservants.

THE JADE EMPEROR

The Chinese pantheon is a diverse mix of Taoist and Buddhist gods. The Jade Emperor is in charge of all life, physical and spiritual. He rules Heaven and presides over a heavenly bureaucracy made up of ministries such as Thunder and Wind, Healing, Wealth, War and Fire run by other gods and spirits.

VIEW OF THE AFTERLIFE
Lady Xin's body was wrapped in 20 layers of silk fabric and robes. Draped over this were two quilts. The outer quilt is embroidered with patterns symbolizing the afterlife and longevity.

Every province, city and town in China has its own guardian deity, each ranked in order of importance. Even within the house there is a god of the bathroom and god of the kitchen. As the Jade Emperor is the supreme Yang, so the Queen Mother of the West is the supreme Yin. She presides over the West—the direction of death and immortality. She is not so much a benevolent as a powerful figure, giving a lively balance to the hierarchy of the Jade Emperor's court.

Emperor of the Eastern Peak
The head of the earthly hierarchy of deities is the Great Emperor of the Eastern Peak, the sacred mountain of T'ai Shan. He represents the authority of the Jade Emperor and ordains when people are born, when they will die and what will be their future. Charms in the name of the Great Emperor are often kept in people's homes to protect them from misfortune. The lesser gods that guard towns and homes are all subordinate to the Great Emperor.

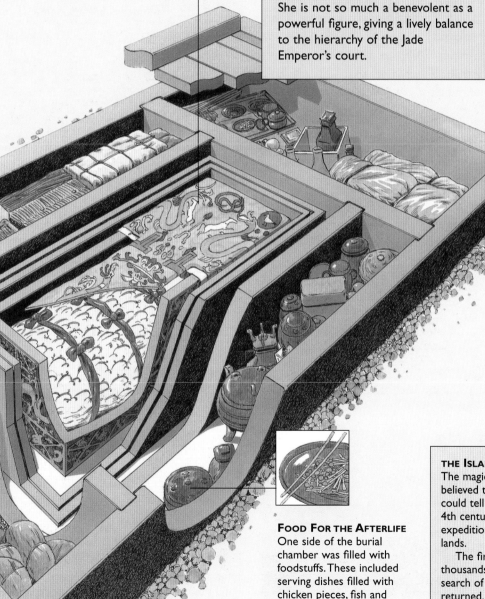

THE P'AN-KU CREATION MYTH
P'an-Ku was born at the moment of separation of Yin and Yang. As Heaven and Earth formed, P'an Ku filled the space between them. He worked for 18,000 years to mould the elements of nature, then died exhausted. But from his body came all life.

His breath became the wind, his voice the thunder, his arms and legs the four directions and five sacred mountains, his blood and semen the rivers and lakes, his muscles and veins the strata of rock and his flesh the soil. His hair became the trees and plants, and his teeth and bones precious metals and gems. His perspiration became the rain, and from his body grew the peoples of the world.

FOOD FOR THE AFTERLIFE
One side of the burial chamber was filled with foodstuffs. These included serving dishes filled with chicken pieces, fish and spareribs; bamboo cases containing eggs and fruit; and jugs of wine.

THE ISLANDS OF THE EASTERN SEA
The magical islands of the Eastern Sea were believed to be home to immortals who could tell the secret of eternal life. From the 4th century B.C., kings were sending expeditions to search for these mythical lands.

The first emperor sent a fleet with thousands of virgins and young men in search of the islands, but they never returned. The emperor believed that the mythical Dragon King was preventing his fleet from reaching the islands and declared war on him. The Dragon King appeared before the emperor, who ordered his archers to shoot at him. That night the emperor died in his sleep.

Keeping Harmony in the World

I n Chinese custom the Emperor became a divine or semi-divine figure who mediated on behalf of the people with Heaven and Earth. Each year he made special sacrifices that required him to fast for three days and go alone to the Temple of Heaven to intercede with the Heavenly Court. By offering sacrifices, he was able to ensure the equilibrium of Yin and Yang and keep the physical and material worlds in harmony.

Maintaining the balance of Yin and Yang through ongoing supplication to the Tao is an essential aspect of Chinese mythology. It is all to do with keeping the balance of creation—of Heaven, Earth, and Humanity—and is considered as relevant today as it ever was. According to Taoist belief, if the balance is disturbed, chaos will result.

The ritual of cosmic renewal
Returning to the Unity is a Taoist ritual aimed at preserving the necessary balance. It takes as its starting point the Five Elements—wood, fire, Earth, metal, and water—which represent the different forms of nature.

From here, by meditation and incantation, the Taoist priest moves up through the Taoist model of reality to the Three, symbolically represented in the human body by the breath, the vital force and the spirit; and from the Three to the Two, namely Heaven and Earth, or Yin and Yang. From the Two he proceeds to the One—the Ch'i—the life breath of the body, which in Chinese thought resides in the head. From here, through meditation, the priest enters the Tao, the Great Oneness from which all comes. With this last step, he reintegrates reality not just for himself but on behalf of everyone.

A Chinese jade ritual disc decorated with dragons, dating from around 300 B.C.

A whimsical interpretation of the myth of Takamori's military prowess, as he attacks the Dragon King's palace under the sea, guarded by fish warriors. Takamori was the last Samurai warrior, from the 19th century.

Astrology and the calendar

The ancient Chinese craft of astrology and calendar-making is concerned with harmonizing human life with the Way of the universe so as to fit into the grand scheme of things. Astrology and horoscopes help individuals to blend into the larger pattern in the manner expressed in the *Tao Te Ching*:

Yielding you overcome,
Bending you are able to stand up again.

The Emperor employed astrologers who determined the times for planting and harvesting and other necessary activities. These sages were scattered throughout the land to signify the role of the Emperor as Humanity's mediator with Heaven.

CONFUCIUS

The Chinese thinker Confucius, whose real name was K'ung, lived in a period when there was much warring between states in China. K'ung encouraged people to hold on to the old ways of behavior.

Hence he is known as a civil servant who seemed concerned mainly with the mundane aspects of correct etiquette. But his interests and influence went far beyond this. He taught about how to live in a peaceful and honest way and found many followers during a time of increasing anarchy.

K'ung believed that the Tao, or the right way to live as an individual, was important if society as a whole were to find peace, and he personally followed Tao teachings. However, his rigid interpretation of the Tao took away its spontaneity and transformed it into a formal set of rules for public virtue.

Confucian morality tales

K'ung's teachings are embodied in 26 morality tales or myths, preserved in Confucian temples. These stories teach selflessness and service and appeared in books for both young and old. In one story, a young woman feeds her husband's toothless grandfather with milk from her breast while her own baby goes without.

Confucius' influence was so great that he was later worshiped as a god.

Magical, Sacred Buildings

The Temple of the White Horse, near Luayang, is claimed to be China's first Buddhist temple. It commemorates the mythical journey of two Buddhist scholars from Afghanistan who brought the Buddhist sutras, or scriptures, to China on a white horse. They came, it is said, in response to emissaries sent by the Emperor Ming around the year 65 A.D., after he had dreamed of a golden man flying in the West. His advisers said that this was the man known in India as the Buddha, who taught how

Potala Palace in Lhasa, Tibet, is the winter residence of the Dalai Lama. Inside, frescos depict episodes from Buddhist myths.

to achieve salvation. From that day, Buddhism began to interact with Taoism and grew in China to have its own distinctive Chinese identity and a role in Chinese mythology and religion.

The Chinese landscape

Temples and monasteries were an essential part of the classical Chinese scenery. Traditional landscape paintings nearly always include a temple or shrine. Today, despite centuries of neglect or destruction, many temples survive. Especially in the hills and mountains time has seemingly stood still amid a magical world of traditional Buddhist and Taoist temples.

Nearly all Chinese temples, whether Taoist, Buddhist, or Confucian, are sited on a north-south axis according to the art of Feng Shui. The temple faces south, the direction of Heaven and the Emperor. Feng Shui literally means "wind and water." It is the recognition that the land itself contains living forces of which we are all a part. Any structure would be placed in accordance with the dynamics of mountain, hill, river, and the shape of the land. Sacred buildings were always given the most auspicious position in the landscape to enhance their appearance.

Evil spirits

The entrance to any sacred building in China says much about the mythology of evil spirits. A false wall was built inside the entrance to deflect evil spirits, which can travel only in straight lines. A water barrier crossed the path, because they cannot cross water, even on a bridge. Finally, door gods would guard the gate.

In Buddhist temples these would be the ferocious Four Heavenly Kings of the four directions, very large figures in full armor bearing weapons. In a Taoist temple there would be two guardians, equally fierce, their faces painted red or green. They might be the Blue Dragon and the White Tiger, or some local deities. The roofs would be adorned with other guardian figures to protect against flying evil spirits. Thus the temple compound is a magical, protected space.

Places of learning

The main function of a Buddhist temple is as a place for teaching, where people can gather to hear the sutras being chanted and recited by the monks. It is a peaceful place, centered on the halls that contain the Buddha in a variety of forms: the Laughing Buddha of the Future, who is usually near the entrance, the Buddha of Compassion, usually in her female form of Kuan Yin, and the three Buddhas of Past, Present, and Future.

When the Buddha is shown in a reclining position, it represents the stage at which he is about to enter nirvana. Buddhists believe people pass through many births in human or other forms. At nirvana, rebirth, disease, suffering, and death cease to exist.

TEMPLES AND MONASTERIES

The Buddhist temple at Pulguksa near Kyongju in South Korea was built in 528 A.D. and reconstructed in the 17th and 20th centuries. It is built on a series of stone terraces and features wooden buildings and walls with tiled roofs. The internal woodwork and eaves of the roofs are beautifully painted with mythological and religious patterns and scenes.

Hall of the Buddha of Pure Earth

Pavilion of the Buddha of Truth

Pavilion of the Buddha called Sakkyamuni

Meditation hall

Pavilion of the Buddha called Amitabha

Bridges of the Lotus and of the Seven Treasures

Main gateway

SHINTO SPIRITUAL HOMES

Shinto shrines are dedicated to the *kami*—folk deities of Japan. The Shinto religion has no founder, dogma or sacred scriptures. The ever-increasing number of folk deities to whom the Japanese believe they are related are revered, rather than a supreme absolute deity. Festivals to honor the folk deities, called *matsuri*, participate at the shrines. Both young and old take part, and hence the Shinto shrine is regarded as the spiritual home of the Japanese.

Shinto shrines are usually found within a sacred grove, and reverence for Nature forms an important part of the Shinto tradition. The shrine is approached through a gateway called a *torii*, signifying entrance to a sacred space.

The Family, Religion, and Politics

FENG SHUI IN THE HOME
The Chinese home will have been planned with the help of a Feng Shui master. For example, the front door will face in the correct direction and the kitchen will be in the correct part of the house. Ensuring the most favorable arrangement on Feng Shui principles, it is believed, will bring good luck and help avoid misfortune.

Among the most noticeable features of Buddhist temples in China are the incense burners. Burning incense symbolizes the constant offerings and prayers made to the deities.

Most Chinese families begin the morning with an offering to the god or goddess of the home. This is a Taoist deity representing the primal force that inhabits the place. The offering may be simply incense or it may include some food, such as tea and cakes. The deity of the home will then placate the deity of the town or city, and so on up the pantheon, like a heavenly bureaucracy. A similar offering may be made to the family ancestors.

Any illness in the family will be treated using traditional Chinese medicine. This derives from Taoism, which teaches that the body is a microcosm for the universe, complete with the many deities whose influence presides over the different parts. Hence, in the human body these elements must be kept in balance, just as in the greater world.

Political control

In modern China religious practice is overseen and controlled by the Communist Party through the Religious Affairs Bureau. There are, for example, restrictions on the number of monks allowed to live in Taoist or Buddhist monasteries. In fact in China, religion has always been controlled by the state, even in the days of the First Emperor in the 2nd century B.C.

Traditionally, religious groups were often the breeding grounds of rebellion in the days of empire, and so the rulers exercised a degree of control over them. The repression of religion and traditional Chinese culture under the present Communist regime has to be seen in this

Female dancers in traditional costume perform at a shrine at the Institute of Confucian Studies in Seoul, South Korea. They are celebrating Confucius' birthday.

context. But now that the Cultural Revolution is long gone, modern China is experiencing some resurgence of sacred life, often involving the rediscovery of forgotten or lost traditions.

Cult of the dead

There is still a thriving cult of the dead in China and all families are expected to take care of their ancestors with ritual offerings. According to Taoism, there are 10 hells, and 18 in Buddhism, each of which subjects its victims to horrific tortures. Because the afterlife frequently involves visits to these hells, families feel a great burden of responsibility to offer atonements for their ancestors.

After death, the body is buried along with offerings for the afterlife. These might include Bank of Hell banknotes, paper cars, paper computers, model houses, and mock gold bars. These can be used by the dead to make hell more bearable and—in keeping with the "heavenly bureaucracy" model—to bribe the officials in hell to release them from some punishments. This aftercare by families goes on for up to seven generations of ancestors. It is one of the strongest and oldest surviving mythical traditions in China.

The dead who do not have anyone to look after them are called Hungry Ghosts, who are said to haunt the world in a state of anxiety and torment. They are greatly feared because of the harm that they may do the living. Chinese people will not go near a burial ground unless it is that of their own ancestors. But once a year, at the Hungry Ghost Festival, efforts are made to placate the ghosts, and Taoist and Buddhist temples compete to accept offerings on behalf of these souls.

Tibetan Buddhists circle Mount Kailash in the Himalayas. The mountain is sacred to both Buddhists and Hindus. Pilgrimages take place throughout the year. Pilgrims make the journey simply because it brings them closer to the divine.

SACRED MOUNTAINS

Tradition has always regarded the mountains of China as sacred. People went there to consult their oracles. Qi Shan, 160 kilometers west of X'ian, was the sacred mountain of the Zhou tribes and the source of the oracles of the *I Ching*. Over time, the site lost its importance, but recently it is being rediscovered and modern fortune-tellers now thrive there.

The greatest of the sacred mountains is Tai Shan, in Shandong Province, with the Yellow River flowing past. It is the home of the fabled Great Emperor of the Eastern Peak, where earthly emperors came to pay their respects. Tai Shan is also worshiped as the mountain of creation, the Origin of Origins. It is believed that from this peak souls enter and leave this world.

There are shrines dedicated to Tai Shan throughout China and Japan, and a stone from the mountain is regarded as a good luck charm.

Pilgrims have been visiting Tai Shan for at least 2,000 years. It is still the most visited of the sacred mountains and in summer the crowds can be enormous. The path that pilgrims climb is itself symbolic of the Way, or the Tao.

CHAPTER 10

NORTH AMERICA

The petroglyph, or rock carving, of Tsagagalal at Horsethief Butte along the Columbia River.

A Rich Legacy and Heritage

The great migrations of peoples to the North American continent very probably occurred between 7,000 and 35,000 years ago. The vast majority of aboriginal peoples came in three different waves of migration from Asia, across a land bridge at the Bering Strait, and south into what are now Canada and the United States. They brought with them their myths and stories, their lore, and their religions.

Much of that rich legacy is still represented in the people themselves: in the many different groups, tribes, and cultures found on the North American continent. Other evidence of this heritage includes artifacts that these early peoples left behind. Jewelry, statues, weapons, and rock art testify to a culture that stretches back for millennia. Many of these artifacts relate directly to myth—the narratives and stories that help shape and maintain a culture's values and beliefs.

The myth of Tsagaglalal—a woman changed into a rock—is directly linked to an actual rock painting, today located above the site of what was once one of the largest indigenous villages in North America. In its heyday, the "Long Narrows" of the Columbia River, in the Pacific northwest of the United States, was home to some 5,000 people. But even by 1805, when the explorers Lewis and Clark arrived, their numbers had dwindled due to the ravages of smallpox and other diseases brought by earlier European traders.

Native Americans formed hundreds of distinct tribes with many different ways of life. But in terms of religious beliefs and myths, there were some 15 cultural areas. Religious ceremonies played an important part in the life of most Native American tribes.

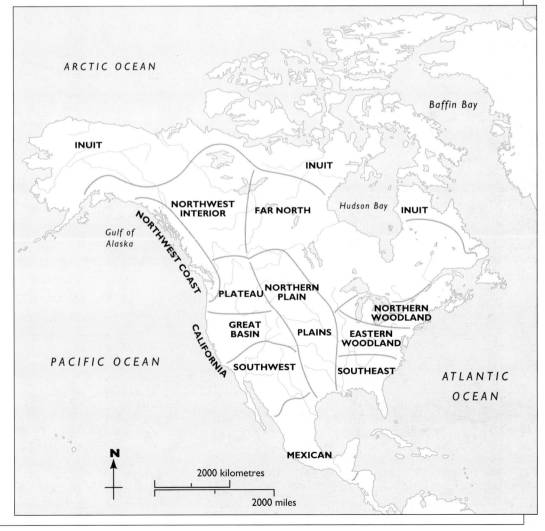

Storytelling and the "Great Spirit"

A Kachina doll of the Hopi of Arizona, representing divine ancestral spirits.

Many of the stories of the early peoples who came to North America from Asia and Eastern Europe reflect elements from those continents or migrations, albeit adapted to the geographical realities of their adopted country. For example, the myths of the Iroquois, who have inhabited the northeastern part of the United States for thousands of years, recall the time when people moved there from some far-off land. This illustrates the tremendous longevity and flexibility of myth, and its seemingly infinite capacity to mold itself to new situations.

The oral tradition

In North America, myths rely heavily on the oral tradition—the passing down of tribal or group stories from one generation to another by word of mouth. Because most groups had no system of formal writing, they developed highly sophisticated methods of narration. Storytelling is usually the province of an elder—a man or woman who is not only highly respected for his or her wisdom, but knowledgeable in the lore of the people. Storytelling can happen informally, for example around a wood stove in the winter, or in a more formal setting marked by ceremony and ritual. Feasts, marriages, and funerals are great opportunities for carrying on the oral tradition and preserving important tribal values.

A bond with the Creator

Characteristic of myth is the notion of a special relationship with the Creator, which is sometimes revealed by the names that are adopted. The nations of the Cheyenne, living in what is now Montana, the Nez Percés in Idaho and eastern Washington State, and the Aleuts of western Alaska, all call themselves "The People," implying that they have been chosen by the Creator for a special purpose. In a creation myth of the Brule Sioux, native to South Dakota, their tribe was rescued from a great flood by an eagle, and charged by the eagle to become a great nation. The eagle carries with it a sense of nobility and hence shows their Creator's special regard for their people.

A 19th-century Navaho blanket based on a sand-painting design. Two supernatural "holy people" flank the sacred maize plant, which is their gift to the mortals.

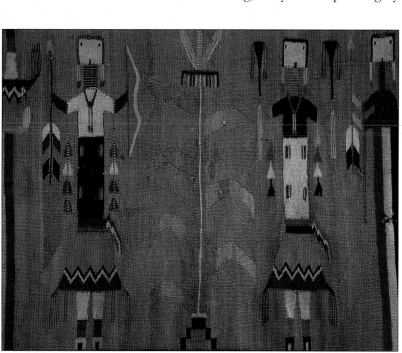

HOW COYOTE MOVED MOUNT ADAMS

In this story, we meet Coyote (Speel-yi), an animal long venerated by and associated with local tribes. Coyote had personally appointed Tsagaglalal to watch over the people.

At this time, Coyote ruled all the land. He had his headquarters down there by the Nch-I-Wana, down by the Bridge of the Gods. Coyote was travelling with his single daughter, and came to the Klickitat country, and he asked if there was a man for his daughter.

"Go see our chief," the people said, "he has plenty of everything and is a great man." Coyote asked, "Who is your chief?" They told him, "Pah-to" [Mount Adams]. So Coyote left his daughter there and went to see Chief Pah-to, who then stood to the north, where the Goat Rocks now stand. Pah-to was a huge mountain, even larger than now. All around were plenty of berries, roots and game. Coyote said to Pah-

to,"""Would you like to marry my daughter?" Pah-to replied with scorn, "I already have a woman I am going to marry. You are too late."

Coyote then said, "All right, that is what I wanted to find out. You will not get any roots, and I will also stop the salmon from coming up the river." Pah-to laughed loud and long. He said, "All right! I am too strong for you. But, if you think that you control me, go ahead and try." Coyote answered, "Yes, I will show you what I can do." Then Coyote moved Pah-to south, dividing the mountain and leaving Goat Rocks undisturbed.

Since then Pah-to has had berries and game, but no roots or salmon.

Wild flowers cover the slopes of Mount Adams in south-western Washington State. The myth of Coyote and Pah-to (Mount Adams) has a double meaning. Not only does it explain why there are no roots or salmon near Mount Adams–which is true–but it delivers the deeper message of warning its audience against unseemly pride.

The bond with the Creator illustrates an important facet of Native American religion and helps to explain the way that the different peoples relate to their environment. Native Americans commonly believe in one great creator god, commonly called the "Great Spirit" or "Great One Above." This deity made the world and everything in it, and in transcendence and creative power comes closest to the western understanding of God. To the Sahaptin peoples, who live in the northwestern interior of the United States, the Creator is known as Nami-Piap, meaning "elder brother," and is worshiped with reverence and familiarity by those groups living along both sides of the Columbia River.

Sanctity of nature

Very important in North American mythology are the animals, ancestors, and other beings whose spirits may inhabit any part of the creation. The Kwakiutl people of the northwest Canadian coast speak freely of the heroic part played by animals in constructing the first totem pole—the pole that "holds up the sky."

This expansive role for animals points to another characteristic of indigenous religion, one consistently upheld by the peoples' mythology—that all of nature is, in the fullest sense, alive. Such beliefs (called animism) extend life, and sometimes even human life, to the whole of creation—rocks, mountains, volcanoes, rivers, everything, in fact.

A World of Myths and Morals

Multnomah Falls, in the Columbia River Gorge, near Portland, Oregon. The waterfall is featured in Native American mythology. It is now part of a national scenic area.

How chipmunks got their stripes, how the rattlesnake acquired its rattle, why salmon swim upstream—mythology offers a ready explanation for most natural phenomena. According to a myth of the Haida people, beavers love to gnaw wood because, long ago, there was a woman who spent more and more time in the water until, finally, she changed into a creature that loved to chew trees and wood.

As in the case of Coyote and Pah-to, the point of these stories is not just to explain nature, but to do so within the context of a world that was created in a certain way, and is maintained and behaves in certain ways. Nature myths reinforce Native Americans' philosophy about the universe, emphasizing the values that are seen to be important.

The "trickster"

Indeed, myths are the foundation for the whole Native American cosmogony—the origins of the universe itself. In the mythology of the Zuni people, who dwell in the pueblos of the southwestern United States, it is the mischievous and overly curious Coyote (Speel-yi) who, in his flawed attempts to steal the light of the Sun and Moon, is responsible for cold entering the world.

This myth is typical in two respects: it answers questions about the way the world is, and it uses an animal as the central character in the telling. The coyote is the "trickster," a creature that possesses certain human qualities—strength, bravery, and guile—along with a flawed nature that predisposes him to mischief. Almost all tribes have a name for this "trickster," and there are usually several myths that feature his ambivalent, yet usually beneficent, nature in action.

A matter of survival

Myths also stress the importance of a close-knit community. In hunter-gatherer societies group cooperation is vital. Narratives that reinforce communal values—sharing, cooperation, harmonious roles for men and women—are needed to help keep a tribe together from generation to generation. The triumph of the Cheyennes in their myth "The Great Race" is due only to the teamwork of the birds that are racing against the Buffalo Woman. The myth has an obvious moral, serving as an object lesson in the importance of work-sharing. In the stark climate of the Great Plains, such a lesson could mean the difference between life and death.

Many other myths also have a moral message. They define what might be called "the good life," often extolling truthfulness or bravery or showing what all the virtues of providing for one's family and respecting one's elders are. When Red Jacket (Sa-go-ye-wat-ha), the great Seneca leader, addressed those who had come to buy the Senecas' lands, he told them the deal was being made "in a crooked manner." To Native Americans, nothing could be more damning.

Tales of courage

Courage is a virtue, says the mythology, that should have universal appeal beyond the male-dominated battlefield. In the Story of Multnomah Falls, a tribal chief's daughter throws herself over a cliff to save her people from a raging epidemic. Here, courage is mixed with sacrificial love. It is just at the point when her lover becomes sick that the girl knows what she must do.

A Native American, dressed for a rain dance, performs at a Pow Wow (social gathering of tribes) at Flagstaff, Arizona.

OUTWITTING THE ENEMY

Both the Native Americans and the ancient Greeks admired guile—the ability to outwit one's enemy—and this is reflected in the mythologies, whether through Coyote or Odysseus.

The haunting howl of the coyote creates a feeling of night-time menace. Coyotes often hunt in packs, stalking prey then defending their kill.

In "Speel-yi Breaks the Dam," Coyote deceives the five Swallow Sisters, and incidentally saves his special people, the Yakamas, by disguising himself as a small baby, to take advantage of the sisters' maternal instincts.

In the Apache myth "Coyote Steals Sun's Tobacco," Coyote again displays his wiliness in outsmarting Sun to obtain tobacco, though in the end he himself is outwitted by the Apaches.

Why Native Americans should respect cunning—and why Coyote should so often come to exemplify it—is not hard to fathom. One thing that humans can certainly learn from the coyote is how to adapt. In North America, despite all the logging, mining and urbanization that has taken place, there are many more coyotes than ever before.

Given the Native Americans' struggle for survival, it is not surprising that such an animal survivor should serve as a role model for them.

At the end of the story, the silvery white mist of the falls serves as a reminder that the purity of the girl's sacrifice was pleasing to the Great Spirit.

To those gathered round to hear such stories, they would have the same impact as modern movies do on their audiences. These myths reinforce key tribal values and yet at the same time share many of the heroic features of classical epics such as *The Odyssey*.

Ritual and Social Life

A ll pre-Columbian North Americans were very spiritual human beings. On rising, they would pray to the "Great Spirit Above" to offer thanks for the new day.

Whenever hunters left to go after game, or root gatherers to look for the tubers of the edible plants, or before the berry pickers touched a huckleberry or blackberry, they would offer up prayers. They prayed not only for success, but for peoples' hearts to be right. They took their creation myths seriously. These stories presented a society that was highly organized both within the individual tribes and families and outside them. People saw themselves as part of an organic whole with the rest of nature, not as part of a hierarchy that was alien to it.

Community spirit

From earliest childhood, the mythic understanding of community plays a prominent part in shaping a Native American's understanding of the world about them. This communal notion remains intact at death. To this day, when a tribal member dies, the reservation to which he or she belonged may "shut down" for the day. It is considered inappropriate to carry on as normal while fellow tribal members "make their journey."

Many rituals mirror that mythic foundation. One of the most significant of these is the "Green Corn Dance" of the Seminole nation. The Dance does much more than simply express gratitude for good crops. It is here that any tribal or clan disputes are settled, rites of purification are conducted and members of tribes from different regions renew their acquaintance.

A Haida totem pole, carved with birds and other animals to represent mythological figures.

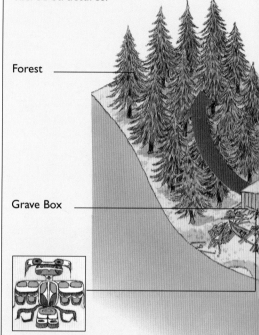

A HAIDA LONGHOUSE

Many myths became "localized" or associated with a certain space, which was sometimes, but not always, deemed sacred. With strong mythic stress on family and community, groups would often construct dwellings where they could relate to or act out some of the myths. Along the northwest coast, where both rainfall and timber were abundant, tribes like the Haida built sophisticated longhouses which were transformed from living spaces to sacred structures.

Forest

Grave Box

GRAVE BOX AND THE SKY WORLD
When Haida died, they were buried in a wooden grave box near the forest, which was on slopes of the coastal mountains. The mountains led to the Sky World, whose chief was the Thunderbird.

FAMILY DWELLINGS
As well as the Haida, other Native Americans constructed dwellings where they could relate to or act out some of the myths. The tribes of the Columbia River desert region, living in an area where wood was scarce, built mat houses for the Washani. The Washani was a strict, traditional religion that rejected any compromise with the old ways.

In the eastern part of Canada and the northeastern United States, tribes also constructed huge hardwood longhouses, some 18 meters in length. These often accommodated extended families, reinforcing the strong familial ties that the tribal myths encouraged.

THE HOUSE AND HEARTH—CENTER OF THE SECULAR AND SACRED WORLDS

The longhouse was symbolically at the center of the universe. Several related families, numbering perhaps 30 or 40 people in all, lived in the house. Each family had its own living area, separated from that of its neighbors by wooden screens or woven mats. A fire was lit at the central hearth for cooking and to keep people warm in winter. People lived mainly off the riches of the sea, although sometimes they went inland to gather berries or to hunt deer and bears.

TRADITIONAL FEASTS

Feasts are an important part of the tradition of myth and ritual among Native Americans. Whereas some may mark essential dates on the calendar of any hunter–gatherer society, such as the First Roots Festival, many others are intended simply to celebrate life.

The feasts pay tribute to the many narratives that extol the joy of living, emphasizing gratitude to the "Great Spirit Above" as a virtue.

Northwest Coast Tribes, such as the Salish and Haida, were famous for their elaborate "Potlatch" feasts. These were designed to showcase the wealth and generosity of the host, and custom indicated that future Potlatches should become more and more generous. Today, many indigenous tribes sponsor events such as "Pow-Wows"—large social occasions that feature traditional costume and Indian dancing, singing and foods. Often a significant amount of time is also devoted to storytelling, whether in a formal or less formal setting.

The Sky World

COSMIC TREE —THE SHAMAN'S POLE

During winter ceremonies, the Haida erected a wooden pole in the center of the longhouse, sticking up through the smoke hole. A shaman climbed this 'cosmic tree' to link the Earth world and the sky world with is spirits and powers.

The Earth World

Souls from the Sea

The souls of the newborn emerged from the sea.

The Underworld

The Earth World

The Underworld

RESPECT FOR THE EARTH

In the past, the absence of "inanimate" objects from Native American religion and myth posed serious problems for indigenous cultures. Many tribal shamans (spiritual leaders) and chiefs preached a return to traditional ways, and the total rejection of agriculture, as advocated by whites. This had the effect of placing many indigenous groups in jeopardy in the 19th century, because the traditional hunter-gatherer existence was scarcely possible any longer because of decreasing numbers of game. Today, however, Indian mythologies and their affinity with the environment may provide the basis for a new ethics of respect for the Earth.

The Sea - home of the whale and source of food

THE UNDERWORLD OF THE SEA

The chief of the underworld was the Whale. The Haida believed that the souls of people to be born emerged from the sea. They carved wooden beams into sea-lion heads, fish, and baleen whales.

Resurgence of Traditions

Recently there has been a revival of interest in Native American traditions both among the peoples themselves and among others. Tribal members are rediscovering their spiritual and mythic heritage. Indigenous groups are once again learning their language, reading their myths in schools, and using storytellers to reinforce tribal and group values. Many non-Native Americans are becoming absorbed in indigenous mythology and customs.

Environmental awareness

Some of this outside interest stems from a new awareness of the environment—a respect for nature that is inherent in Native American culture. Some is the result of a trend toward alternative forms of spirituality. The combination of these factors has produced the "eco-religions."

Some of these are newly created, others claim ties to ancient religions, but they all connect significant portions of their practice to the sacredness of the Earth. Many bookshops in the United States have books about connecting with one's ancestors, conducting "chanting ceremonies" and other spiritual practices long associated with the religion and mythology of the indigenous peoples of North America.

A member of the Red Thunder Stoney Indian professional dance group performs at Buffalo Nations Pow-Wow at Banff National Park, Canada.

HUMOR AND SEX IN MYTH

A notable feature of Native American myth is its unabashed willingness to explain human beings, warts and all. Whether by the mention of a patch of woods that takes its name from its resemblance to patches of body hair, or a graphic description of the sexual act, indigenous mythology does not shrink from affirming sex and procreation as vital to a group's continued existence. Hand in glove with that is the love of humor—sometimes ribald and earthy, but always present. At times, humor is employed to make a moral lesson more palatable, but in others, it is simply an appreciation of the basic human drives.

An Iroquois wears a fright mask and stands in the doorway of a traditional sacred longhouse.

Commercial exploitation

Understandably, many Native American leaders are unhappy with what they perceive as the commercialization and debasement of their sacred traditions by ignorant outsiders. For example, some American holiday resorts offer their guests the use of a sweat lodge—a deeply religious ritual sacred to Native Americans. Sacred objects employed in indigenous religious ceremonies can be bought in some shops. Indian leaders understand that most of the interest in their traditions is not commercially motivated, but they are worried that much is being taken out of its sacred context and turned into "home remedies" in a culture looking for easy answers.

What is undoubtedly true is that the mythologies of North America have moved to the mainstream. This shift has allowed more people to hear these stories and to experience their power for themselves. While religious myths should always be viewed with respect, and in the context of their tradition, their wider currency is a positive sign for the appreciation of spiritual traditions and religious tolerance as a whole.

Mohawks demonstrate drumming to a non-Native American audience as part of a traditional ritualistic spirituality relating to nature.

SWEAT LODGE CEREMONY

The "sweat lodge" highlights the Native American belief in the connections between the spiritual and the physical realms. Ideally located near running water, the lodge is constructed out of branches overlaid with blankets, hides, or earth. It stands about 1–1.5 meters high, and resembles a beehive. Rocks heated on a fire are placed in the middle, and the participants are seated in a ring.

Almost all North American tribes have a story about the origins and sacredness of the Sweat Lodge ceremony. The stories may differ in the details, but they agree on the divine origins of the ceremony, and on the strong religious nature of the ritual.

Usually the "Water-Pourer" (who is sometimes a tribal shaman) is in charge, and decides how to interpret the many rules governing the ceremony. Some traditions do not allow women to participate; others admit non-menstruating women; others still, will not allow non-Native American participants, but some will if they have indigenous sponsors.

In all traditions, a respectful demeanor is required of the participants, as would be expected in a church. Once inside the lodge, the leader begins the ceremony with a ritualistic prayer of thanksgiving, usually combined with a brief recitation of how the sweat lodge was given to the tribe. The ceremony can last from a few

minutes up to a few hours, during which time the leader employs chants and prayers to ask that the peoples' hearts might be made right; that the tribe's members be blessed, as they strive to live properly. Sometimes the participants repeat the chants.

At certain times during the ceremony, the leader pours water (perhaps mixed with evergreen needles or other aromatic foliage) over the hot rocks, causing a fragrant blast of hot steam to rise into the darkness of the Lodge. Traditionally, the "sweat," as the ceremony is called, ends with a prayer of blessing for all those who took part, asking that the Great Spirit guide and protect them.

Normally, at no time are people allowed to pass between the fire and the other participants—they enter and exit the ceremony by the door, then make their way around the edge of the lodge. After the ceremony, the participants plunge into cold water or roll in nearby snowdrifts.

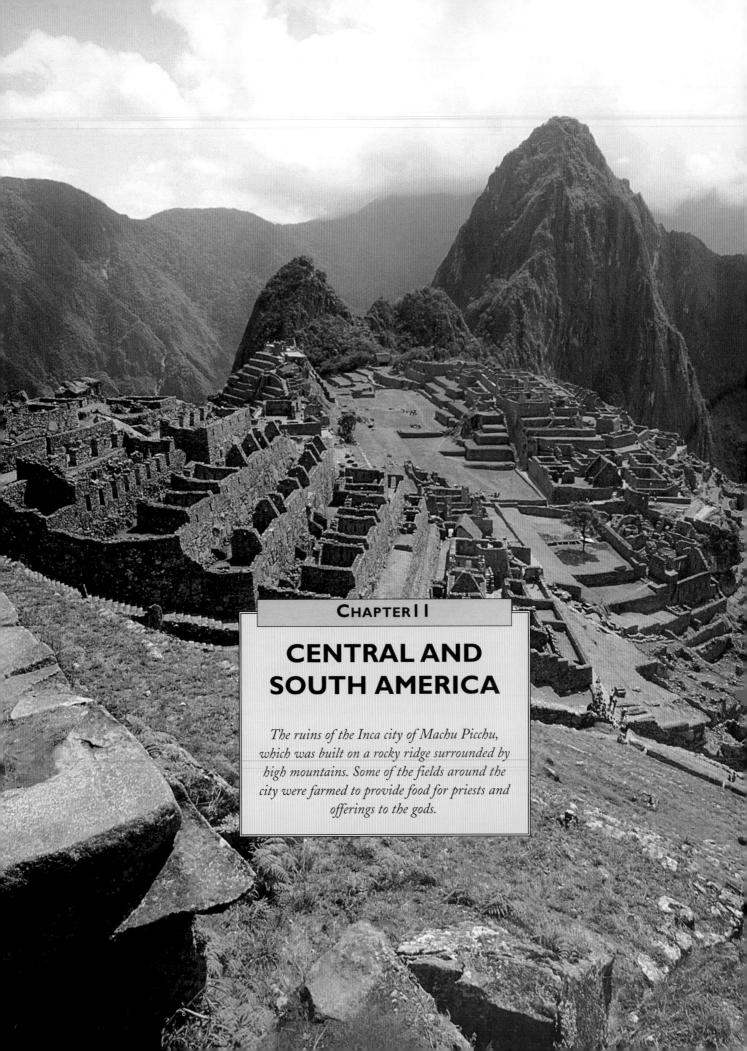

CHAPTER 11

CENTRAL AND SOUTH AMERICA

The ruins of the Inca city of Machu Picchu, which was built on a rocky ridge surrounded by high mountains. Some of the fields around the city were farmed to provide food for priests and offerings to the gods.

From the Writings of Explorers

The Inca empire of South America extended along the Andes mountain range for over 5,500 kilometers: from south of present-day Colombia, through Ecuador, Peru and Bolivia to the north of Chile and Argentina, and from the desert of the Pacific coast in the west to tropical forest on the eastern flank of the mountains.

Spanish conquerors

The Inca called their realm Tawantinsuyu, "The Land of the Four Quarters." Their capital was Cuzco, a city in the mountains of southern Peru. The empire was at its height when, in 1532, it was conquered by Francisco Pizarro and a small band of Spaniards, who happened to arrive during a civil war. One of the main attractions of the Inca empire for the Europeans was its vast wealth of gold and silver. To the Incas, gold was sacred to the Sun, and silver to the Moon. Knowledge of the Inca has come largely from the writings of the early Spanish colonizers of the Andes.

The Inca were not the first civilization to populate the Andean region. Remains of ceremonial centers in the area date back to almost 2000 B.C. The Inca were comparative latecomers. They arrived sometime after the Tiwanaku and Huari civilizations of the Altiplano and Central Peruvian regions respectively. The major phase of Inca expansion did not take place till the century before the Spanish arrived. Some of the earlier Andean peoples were more technologically innovative than the Inca, but the Inca excelled in statecraft, organization, and administration.

Empires of Central America

In Central America, to the north, the most important pre-Hispanic civilizations were the Aztecs and the Maya. The Aztecs ruled most of what is now Mexico, before the coming of the Spaniards. The Maya, who held sway earlier than the Aztecs, lived in parts of present-day Guatemala, southern Mexico, and northern Honduras. Mayan mythologies have been recorded. The Maya wrote in hieroglyphics in parchment books, some of which were translated by Spanish scribes of the colonial period.

The focal points of Central and South American mythologies are the major towns and cities of the Aztec, Maya and Inca civilizations that existed prior to the arrival of European explorers in the late 16th and early 17th centuries. There were other great civilizations before this time, such as the Chimu, Tiwanaku, and Nazca, but there are no written records of their mythologies.

Inca Society and City Life

The Inca regarded their capital city Cuzco as the navel of their empire. Boundaries starting from Cuzco's main square divided their realm into quarters: Collasuyu, the Altiplano (high plain) of the south; Antisuyu, eastward toward the Amazon basin; Cuntisuyu, the dry Pacific coastal region; and Chinchaysuuyu, extending northward through Peru and into present-day Ecuador.

The Inca universe
Other divisions within the Inca state were dual. The Inca nobility was split between the royal lineages of *hanan*, or upper Cuzco, and *hurin*, or lower Cuzco. Duality reflected the way that the Inca understood their universe: as a series of balances between opposing, but complementary forces, with Cuzco poised between lowland desert and tropical jungle on either side of the Andes mountains.

Social divisions
The Inca ruler, or *Sapa Inca*, was recognized as the pre-eminent lord throughout the empire. He headed the royal lineages, and was expected to take his sister as a wife. The mass of the population was

The Inca used khipu *to record details. Whether or not* khipu *were used to record verbal, as well as numerical, data remains undetermined, but there is some evidence that suggests they were used to record histories and legends.*

Incas offer sacrifices of maize and llamas to the spirits of the mountain—a copy of a drawing of 1565 by Spaniard Felipe Guaman Poma de Ayala.

Another drawing by Guaman Poma shows Inca venerating their dead, taking mummies from tombs and parading them on litters.

INCA DEITIES

The Inca had many gods. Even the emperor was treated as a god. He was believed to be descended from the Sun. In Cuzco, in the Temple of the Sun, the Inca's most sacred shrine, the emperor, priests, and important officials regularly worshiped the gods.

Viracocha

The creator god who made the universe and all the natural and supernatural beings in it. He is often described as a white-skinned, bearded man in a long robe and with the tonsure of a priest. His appearance led many Spaniards to believe either that their arrival had been foretold, or that long ago some Christian saint had preached in the Andean region.

Inti

The Sun, considered to be the male divine ancestor of the Inca lineage. He was associated with the metal gold and was the focus of much official worship. The main festival in his honor was *Inti Raimi*, which marked the winter solstice.

Killa

The Moon, the female divine ancestor of the Inca. She was associated with the metal silver. According to myth, when the Sun and Moon were first created, the Moon was the brighter of the two. This made the Sun jealous, so he threw ashes in her face, making her darker, as she appears today.

Illapa

The god associated with thunder and lightning. According to Guaman Poma, when sacrifices were made to this deity, the Inca people would burn coca plants and offerings of food. They would also abstain from eating salt and having sexual intercourse. During the colonial period, Illapa became associated with the Christian Saint James (Santiago).

huaca (pronounced 'waka')

A general term for shrines, objects of veneration, holy places, and the supernatural forces associated with them. Mountains, lakes, trees, and unusual rock formations could all be *huaca*, as were specific places associated with myths and legends.

ancestors

Mummified ancestors, particularly those of past Inca rulers and heads of lineages, were revered in Inca society. When an important person died, the body would not be buried. It would be kept, embalmed and dressed in the finest woven cloth. This custom appalled the invading Spaniards.

divided by age into a series of subgroups, according to their work capability. Lands that were incorporated into the Inca empire paid taxes not in money or goods, but in the form of work or services. This included agricultural labor and military service. To ensure a subject community's compliance and good behavior, its principle religious idol was held as hostage in Cuzco. In the case of populations that were persistently troublesome, whole communities would be relocated far away.

The First Inca People

A re-enactment of the emergence from Lake Titicaca of Manco Capac and Mama Ocllo, the supposed founders of Cuzco, the Inca capital.

Sources of Inca mythology do not always agree in every detail. This is possibly because the Inca empire was made up of diverse peoples, but also perhaps because of the motivations of the people transcribing the myths. The mythological founding of Cuzco is an example.

The Inca Garcilaso de la Vega, the son of a Spanish nobleman and an Inca princess, relates how, in olden times, before the Incas, the people lived without religion or government. They did not build houses or know how to cultivate the earth. The Sun took pity on these poor people. He sent down to Earth one of his sons and one of his daughters to teach the people how to live, and to respect him as their divine ancestor.

The two children of the Sun emerged from Lake Titicaca, with instructions to wander wherever they wished, and to sink a golden rod into the earth whenever they stopped to rest. At the chosen place where they were to make their settlement, the rod would sink into the Earth to its full length at the first blow.

The founding of Cuzco

The two wandered far and wide, always trying to sink their rod into the Earth, but never succeeding, until they came at last to the vale of Cuzco. There, on the mountain known as Huanacauri, the staff sank into the Earth with just one thrust and they knew that they had found the chosen place. The savages of the area saw the newcomers, adorned and clothed by the Sun, and began to worship them as Children of the Sun,

The Moche people inhabited the northern coast of Peru between the 1st and 7th centuries A.D. This Moche inlaid ornament depicts a bird-headed human diety.

Niches in the walls of the fortress of Sacsahuaman in Cuzco were built to remind the Inca of the caves from which they believed their ancestors emerged.

and to obey them as kings. The pair founded the city of Cuzco, divided into upper and lower parts, and became the first Inca and Coya (empress), known as Manco Capac and Mama Ocllo.

An alternative version

In Sarmiento de Gamboa's possibly more authentic account, there are not just one brother and sister, but four of each. They all emerged from a cave on mountain called Tambotoco, six leagues (30 kilometers) from Cuzco. De Gamboa mentions the first Inca and Coya, Manco Capac and Mama Ocllo, as well as a sister called Mama Guaco, who was a great warrior, and two brothers who turned to stone. One of these became the most important *huaca* of the Inca realm, the other a sacred boundary marker.

VIRACOCHA THE CREATOR

Pedro de Sarmiento de Gamboa, who was commissioned to write a history of the Inca for the Spanish viceroy, tells of a creation that took place in stages.

Firstly, the god Viracocha created the world, which was dark, without Sun, Moon, or stars. Then he created a race of giants, but decided that they were too large, and instead created men of his own size, like those of today. But they lived in darkness.

Viracocha intended that the people he had created should know him and serve him. However, after a while, they started to develop the vices of greed and arrogance. He became angry with them and turned some to stone. Others were swallowed up by the earth, or by the sea. He then sent a flood, called a pachakuti, *which means "a turning around of the world." It rained for 60 days and 60 nights, leaving hardly any trace of the* landscape and living things that had been before.

After the flood, Viracocha decided once more to populate the world, only this time to make it more perfect. He went to an island in Lake Titicaca, and there ordered that the Sun, Moon, and stars should emerge. Virachocha then left the island and went to the ancient ruins of Tiwanaku, where he drew on stones the peoples of the various nations he wished to create.

He then traveled the land, ordering the people to appear. Some emerged from lakes, some from springs, others from valleys, caves, trees, stones, and mountains. These people multiplied and formed the different peoples of the Andean region.

Inca Worship

The state religion of the Inca Empire was the cult of the Sun, the male ancestor of the Inca royal lineage. The center for religious worship was the temple of Coricancha in Cuzco, which astonished the conquering Spaniards with its wealth in gold. Not only were the walls of the temple lined with gold, but according to the Spanish chronicler Pedro de Cieza de León, inside, a herd of more than 20 golden llamas grazed with their young, watched over by golden shepherds with golden slings.

The temple of Coricancha was in the form of a courtyard with a single entrance, around which were six chambers. One of these was dedicated to Inti—the Sun. This was richly covered with gold and contained Inti's image. Another chamber, decorated with silver, was dedicated to the Moon, and there was a chamber for the thunder god, Illapa. Coricancha temple also held the religious objects and treasures from the conquered provinces, which were permanently kept in the imperial capital.

In many parts of South America, people honour the dead on the eve of 2 November. The Aztecs believed that all spirits met on this night to worship the devil and the Lord of Death.

An Inca observatory

As well as being a center for worship, the temple was the center of a cosmic dial for tracking celestial movements and correlating these with features of the landscape. Forty-one sighting lines, called *ceques*, radiated from the enclosure toward the horizon. Along these lines were located 328 *huacas*, or sacred sites, which probably represented the days in 12 lunar months. The *ceques* might have been grouped into upper and lower sets, corresponding to the divisions of Cuzco, and into groups corresponding to the four quarters of the Empire. At least one of the lines, it is believed, was related to movements of the Milky Way.

The role of the ancestors

From early times in the Andes, a group's ethnic identity was given by its ancestors. The group's name would often be that of a founding father. The corpses of the ancestors were among the group's most sacred possessions. Andean societies did not draw a rigid distinction between the living and the dead. The dead, it was believed, continued to influence the health and well-being of their descendants, and were consulted whenever important decisions were taken.

Techniques of embalming and mummification developed early in Andean civilization. By the time of the Inca, mummies were regarded as quasi-living beings, were richly clothed and were attended at special shrines. Mummies of the deceased Inca rulers were particularly important, and ceremonies of the Inca court would emphasize their human characteristics. They were served food and drink in the morning and evening, and would spend the day in a round of public activities.

Celebrating the Inti Raimi festival at the fortress of Sacsayhuaman. Men dressed in costume to represent the Inca carry a Sun disc and skeletons on litters.

HUMAN SACRIFICE

On the accession of a new Inca, every province of the four quarters of Tawantinsuyu would send sacrificial offerings to the Inca capital. These would include llamas and alpacas, woven textiles, and precious metals as well as children.

In Cuzco, the Inca received the gifts in the main plaza. The children walked around the statues of the Creator, the Sun, the Moon and Thunder, circling them twice. The Inca then called the priests of the provinces, and had them divide the sacrifices into four parts, corresponding to the four quarters of the Inca realm.

The children were then told to leave the capital, not by the roads they had come by, but along the *ceques*. They traveled in straight lines through ravines and over mountains, until each one reached a designated *huaca*. This sacred place was probably associated with the particular child's lineage or province. There the child would be sacrificed, sometimes by suffocation, sometimes the child's heart would be ripped out and the face of the *huaca* anointed with the child's blood.

The Living and the Dead

Homage to Mother Earth

The Quechua- and Aymara-speaking peoples of the Andean region today see nature as animate and dynamic. Rocks, mountains, and water sources are all "alive" and all can influence the lives of human beings. These and the Pachamama (Mother Earth) receive regular offerings of corn beer, alcohol, and coca leaves when agricultural and other festivities take place.

August—the month of the Pachamama—is considered particularly important throughout the Andean region. On the first day of August the landscape is thought to be very alive, and in many parts it is forbidden to disturb the Earth by working it, collecting firewood or mining. Libations are made the night before, when it is said that at midnight the mineral veins crossing the mountains glow or burn.

A lasting legacy of Inca times is that ancestors still play an important part in the lives of Andean people. The Christian festivals of All Saints and All Souls have become important as the Day of the Dead throughout Latin America. On the first days of November, Andean people make ceremonial visits to the cemeteries to honor their deceased relatives. They may prepare special foods for them, including bread baked in the shape of people, animals, and ladders to help them ascend to heaven. In the Andean region the Day of the Dead coincides with the start of the rainy season, so the dead are associated with the coming of the first rains.

Help from the dead

In Sud Lípez, in southern Bolivia, people see their relationship with their ancestors as being a reciprocal one. Before an important festival, such as marking a family's llama herd, they perform a ritual in which the dead, who are symbolically present are offered water, corn beer, and alcohol to drink. It is said that the dead are always thirsty. In return, the dead are asked to help the living with llama herding activities in the year ahead. A similar ritual is performed before other festivals, such as a llama sacrifice for the good of a mine, or before the Day of the Dead, when the ritual is reckoned to help the dead on their journey to heaven.

A masked dancer at the Virgin Del Carmen festival in Peru. The word "Virgin" (Spanish -Virgen) is used by many Qhechua-speaking communities to refer to the Pachamama. So it is ambiguous whether the festival is for the Catholic saint or the Andean deity.

CEREMONIAL DRUNKENNESS

Ritual intoxication plays an important part in some ceremonies in which offerings are made to the Earth and mountain spirits. The participants are seated in a particular order, and are served huge quantities of alcohol by appointed servers. On receiving a cup, the drinker is expected to pour a few drops of the liquid onto the ground, for the Pachamama, before consuming the remainder. Ritual drunkenness has been important in the Andes since before the arrival of the Spaniards. It was one of the customs that horrified the Spanish clergy of the colonial regime.

Once or twice a week, Bolivian tin and silver miners in the mines of Potosi will gather round the statue of the mine Devil, Tío, presenting him with coca leaves, alcohol, and cigarettes.

In ancient Cuzco, festivals and ceremonies invariably were held out of doors. At a re-enactment a woman makes an offering to the Sun god.

THE MINER'S DEVIL

The southern Andean region that is now Bolivia has been known for its mineral wealth since before the Spanish invasion. The silver mines of Potosí were a major source of riches for the imperial coffers of the Spanish empire. More recently the region has been known for its tin production.

Bolivian tin miners make offerings to a figure that is in the form of the Devil. He is known as the Tío (literally "Uncle") or Supay. In Quechua, the Inca language, "Supay" denoted the souls of the dead. The term was later adopted by colonial priests in their efforts to translate the concept of the Devil for their Quechua congregations. The idea of the Devil being found in mines recalls both the Christian Hell being underground and the Andean hidden or inner world of *manqha pacha*, the abode of wild supernatural forces such as the mountain spirits.

The Devil of the mines is not necessarily evil. He can be a friend to the miners, helping to make them rich through the discovery of new veins of metal. But he can also become angry if he does not receive his due offerings.

Many miners will talk to him, explaining their problems, needs and worries. Once or twice a year, he may also receive a llama, sacrificed to ensure the continuing good fortune of the mine. Without these offerings, Tío might cause a fatal accident or cause a mineral vein to disappear.

The Empire of the Sun

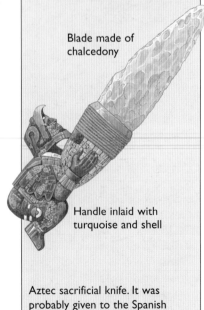

Blade made of chalcedony

Handle inlaid with turquoise and shell

Aztec sacrificial knife. It was probably given to the Spanish conqueror Cortés, who sent it back to the Emperor Charles V in Europe.

F ew ancient civilizations match the splendor and magnificence that belonged to the Aztec empire of southern Mexico. The Aztecs claimed to be descended from nomadic peoples from northern Mexico. They came to the Lake Texcoco region in 1300 A.D. and their empire lasted until 1521.

In all the Americas, only the Inca of Peru surpassed the Aztecs in terms of size of empire. Nevertheless, the Aztecs were unequalled in their expansive trading networks, diverse agricultural economy and elaborate religious beliefs. They worshiped hundreds of gods and goddesses, each one having his or her own sphere of authority or power. Religion dominated the Aztec culture, showing just how powerful myths can be.

The plumed serpent

Although the common people had many different shrines to their different gods, the main god in pre-Columbian mythology was Quetzalcoatl. Quetzalcoatl was often depicted as a plumed serpent, but he was also linked with other natural phenomena, such as the sky. He also served to provide heavenly sanctions for earthly activities such as learning and civilization.

According to the Aztecs' creation myth, the two creator gods, Ometecuhtli ("Lord of the Duality") and Omeciuatlé ("Lady of the Duality"), made the entire universe, including the Sun, the other gods, human beings, and the Earth. They were far removed from Aztec society, however, and lived in the 13th level of heaven. It was the younger gods whose mythology drove Aztec society and created the notorious system of ritualistic human sacrifice.

BLOOD SACRIFICE

Human sacrifice was the most important feature of Aztec ritual. The Aztecs saw themselves as "the People of the Sun," whose duty it was to wage perpetual war and feed the Sun with the hearts and blood of their victims.

The Aztec priest and his helpers, dressed all in black, took the victims to the sacrificial altar. Normally, the victims would be tied or held down across the altar to prevent them from escaping. But in the case of voluntary warrior sacrifice, the victims would remain both still and silent while a priest cut open their chests and took out their hearts. The hearts were offered to the Sun God and then burned in a stone urn.

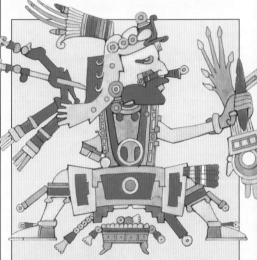

GODS OF CREATION

One of the most important Aztec gods was Huitzilopochotli ("Hummingbird of the South"), the god of war and storms. As shown above, he carried a weapon in his left hand, and his head and left leg were decorated with hummingbird feathers. He was also linked with the Sun-god Tonatiuh, and was reborn every day.

In the sequence on the right, Huitzilopochotli prepares to rise in the morning. He has the Sun-serpent on his back, helping him to push the Moon and Stars out of the way. At the noonday zenith, he reigned supreme over the sky. Later the Cihuateteo, a group of divine women, escorted the Sun down through the western sky and into the kingdom of darkness. This was the territory of Tezcatlipoca, god of the night sky.

Pyramid of Quetzalcoatl
The Toltec people created an empire in Mexico around 900–1200 A.D. They were warlike, believed in witchcraft, and performed human sacrifices to their gods. Around 1000 A.D., they took over the Maya city of Chichén Itzá and built a pyramid to its first leader, Quetzalcoatl, whom they revered as a god.

THE SOLAR DEITY
The Sun had to be kept moving through the sky. To ensure this happened, human blood had to be offered up in a daily stream of sacrifices.

TONATIUH
At noon the Sun god Tonatiuh is hot and thirsty. He must be fed with hearts and blood or he would burn up and the universe would disappear.

TEZCATLIPOCA
A deity of many forms, he was the original Sun who was thrown out of the sky and became the god of the night sky.

The Demon of the night

The Sun-serpent with Huitzilopochotli

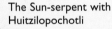

After the blood-letting, the Sun can rise again.

HUITZILOPOCHOTLI

He was both the Sun and the young warrior who was born each day, journeyed through the sky and met his own death and resurrection at night.

CIHUATETEO
Cihuateteo was both the mother god and a group of divine women who escorted the Sun from its zenith to its death at night. After dark they attacked travelers and struck them down with palsy.

The Mayan and Amazonian Legacy

The classic period of Mayan civilization lasted from about 300–900 A.D. During that time, the great temples of Palenque, Tikal, and Copán were built—a legacy that has made Mayan civilization famous for its art and architecture. Swamps were drained and trees were cleared to make way for intensive cultivation. Numerous hieroglyphic texts were sculpted in stone, painted on pottery, or written in ink on long strips of parchment, which were then folded to make books.

The Maya civilization declined at the end of the classic period, almost certainly because of overpopulation and environmental degradation.

The "all-seeing" book
According to Maya mythology, the first human beings to be created could see everything under the sky and on the Earth. The gods, however, decided to limit human sight to what was obvious and nearby. The lords of the Quiché Maya people had the means to overcome this human short-sightedness. This was called an *ilbal*—a "seeing instrument"—with which they could know about events in the distant past or future. It was in the form of a book.

The lords of Quiché consulted their book whenever they sat in council. They called it Popol Vuh ("Council Book"). The book gave an account of the forefathers of their lineages, of the times before the first sunrise and of the first rising of the Sun, Moon, and morning star.

The Olmec people preceded the Maya and Aztecs in Mexico. They made carvings of rulers and supernatural beings.

Transcribing Mayan languages

By the 16th century, many Mayan sites had been abandoned or taken over by other peoples, but some of the hieroglyphic books survived. Spanish missionary priests burned many of these books. However, some priests worked out how to adapt the European alphabet to the sounds of the Mayan languages. Some indigenous peoples, notably the surviving members of the lineages of the Quiché kingdom, learned to use alphabetic writing to make alphabetic copies of their ancient books, including the Popol Vuh.

In the early 18th century, a friar named Francisco Ximénez laid his hands on one of these copies, noted down the Quiché script and added a Spanish translation. This document has survived to this day, and is a major source of knowledge about Mayan mythology. Today, many Mayan sites are being restored.

HOW FOOD WAS FIRST GROWN

A myth from the Trio people of Surinam and Brazil tells of the origin of horticulture.

The culture hero Paraparawa went fishing. At first he caught nothing, but eventually he landed a small fish called Waraku. Suddenly, the fish became a woman. The woman told Paraparawa that she wanted to see his village.

Waraku was surprised when she saw the village, and asked Paraparawa "Where is your food? Where is your house? Where is your drink?"

Paraparawa replied that he had no house, and that his bread was the soft pith of the waruma reed. As they returned to the water, the woman said, "Wait. My father is coming and he is bringing bananas,

yams, sweet potatoes, and yuccas."

Paraparawa saw first the leaves of the yucca plant emerging from the water. Then he saw the red eyes of Waraku's father, as he had arrived in the form of an alligator. Paraparawa was frightened and ran away. The woman, however, took the food plants and gave them to Paraparawa.

She told him how to plant them by clearing a field and, when they had all grown, she showed him what was needed to make bread from the yucca, and how to cook food. Paraparawa grew used to the new foods and stopped eating the pith of the waruma reed.

SHAMANISM AND THE SPIRIT WORLD

In many Amazonian societies the shaman combines the roles of politician, religious leader and healer.

Among the Yanomami people of Venezuela and Brazil, a shaman will inhale hallucinogenic powders, made from plants that grow in the forest, to induce a trance. This then enables him travel to the spirit world. One of the main purposes of the shaman's work is to heal the sick. The Yanomami do not regard illness and death as having natural causes. They believe sickness is brought about by demons who capture the soul of the sufferer, sometimes after it has been delivered to them by the shamans of an enemy community. The shaman's job is then to restore the soul to the sufferer.

A shaman in Amazonia collects plants from the forest for medicinal uses.

CHAPTER 12

OCEANIA

An Aboriginal bark painting depicting termites, from Arnhem Land, Northern Territory, Australia. In the "Dreamtime," ancestral beings take on forms that include all kinds of insects, reptiles, and birds.

Peoples of Oceania

KITH AND KIN

Throughout Oceania the most important social element is that of kinship. Its societies are organized around related kin groups, and these often prescribe who should marry whom, and how people should behave towards one another. Sometimes, traditional law requires them to avoid each other: in many places a man is legally bound to avoid his mother-in-law. Often aunts and uncles will also be called "Mother" or "Father" and will share parental responsibilities. Compared to many parts of the world, Oceanic societies are small in scale, and people have close ties to each other and to their land.

Oceania is aptly named, covering a huge expanse most of which is ocean, with many of its peoples living on island archipelagos scattered across the Pacific Ocean and Coral Sea. It comprises three main areas: Australia and Melanesia, which includes Papua New Guinea and the nearby island groups; Micronesia—thousands of tiny islands including the Marianas, the Marshall Islands and Kiribati (formerly the Gilbert Islands); and Polynesia, which encompasses New Zealand (or Aotearoa), Tonga, Samoa, and Tahiti, and the far-flung islands of Hawaii and Easter Island.

Waves of migrants

The population of Oceania is varied, and hundreds of different languages are spoken. The first arrivals were the Aboriginal Australians: Stone Age hunter-gatherers who reached the continent more than 50,000 years ago. They probably traveled down from Asia during the last Ice Age. The land masses were very different then, and they could have walked right down the Malay Peninsula and crossed from Papua New Guinea into Australia. Aboriginal society was—and still is—very egalitarian. Leadership was provided by male and female elders who "held the Law" for their communities.

Between 3,000 and 7,000 years ago, fresh waves of migrants moved down through Indonesia. Traveling by canoe, they spread through Oceania, using the islands as stepping stones. The most adventurous of them traversed vast expanses of ocean to reach the Polynesian islands. These societies lived mainly by fishing, but they kept pigs and poultry and made temporary food "gardens." They were more hierarchical than the Aboriginal hunter-gatherers, having chiefs, "big men," and, in the Solomon islands, very powerful "noble" classes. Most also had warriors who regularly engaged in warfare with other groups.

Where the three main regions of Oceania meet there is a mixing of cultures and myths.

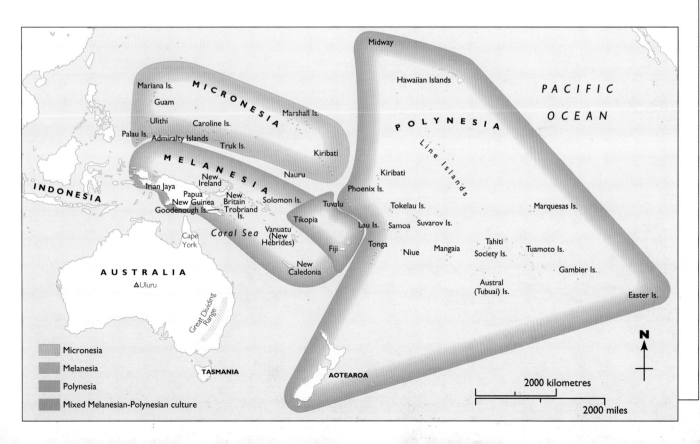

Micronesia
Melanesia
Polynesia
Mixed Melanesian-Polynesian culture

In the Beginning

MANA FROM HEAVEN
The idea that mythological ancestors remain as a form of spiritual power appears in many guises in Oceania. One of the most familiar is the notion of *mana*, a Polynesian term which, like the Maori word *hau*, refers to the cosmological power that may be held by certain people, or in sacred objects. The "dark side" of such power—that the ancestral forces can be very dangerous—is conveyed by words such as *tabu*, which is common throughout much of Oceania.

Ulhuru (Ayers Rock) in the Central Desert of Australia, is one of Oceania's most sacred sites. The Aborigines believe the rock is infused with the creative powers of their ancestors.

The mythologies of Oceania are as varied as its peoples, but there are some common themes. Most center on a primordial era in which ancestral beings made the world, often from their own bodies, and became the ancestors of the human clans that followed.

Living ancestors
Once they had performed their creative deeds, these ancestors did not go away: they settled down, staying invisibly inside the land or sea, or in waterholes, trees, or stones. In this way, the whole environment remained animated—alive with their spiritual essence. The landscape is seen as being wide awake, watching and judging human actions, helping people by providing food and nurture, or punishing those who transgress ancestral laws.

As well as keeping an eye on human behavior, the ancestral beings are often an essential part of how Oceanic societies are organized. Traditionally, each group—and so each individual—is linked with a particular ancestral totem. In Australia

and much of Melanesia, these totems include birds, fish, snakes, and other animals, as well as thunder, floodwaters, or other elements. Mythology is thus integral to personal identity and the organization of social life. In Polynesia and Micronesia the mythology focuses upon fewer, "big" gods, but there are still many important ancestral deities.

Calling on the ancestors
Many Oceanic societies still perform rituals that are believed to bring the ancestral forces into the visible world. Often these are "increase" rituals, whereby the ancestors are asked to provide help or boost resources. Sometimes they require sacrifices, but more often they rely upon the calling forth of ancestral power through songs, dances, and enactments of ancestral deeds. Such rituals open the door to a sacred domain that is never very far away.

Keeping the myths alive
Traditionally, the myths of Oceania were recorded through oral storytelling and formal recitations. This ensured that they were passed from one generation to the next. People also painted scenes from the stories on rocks and bark, and carved stone and wooden sculptures of ancestral beings. They protected their ancestral places with laws and ceremonies.

In many Oceanic societies the myths are still sacred, and people are progressively initiated into their deeper levels of meaning at different stages of their lives. Sometimes, the most secret "inner" stories are known only to a few of the oldest people. As a result, elders are treated with great respect, because they hold the most sacred knowledge.

Such methods of keeping mythology alive have persisted for millennia. Rock art in some parts of Oceania has been carefully maintained for many thousands of years, and there are numerous myths that seem to refer to the floods that followed the last Ice Age. Today, people are also photographing and videotaping ceremonies, and writing down their myths to make sure that this heritage is not lost.

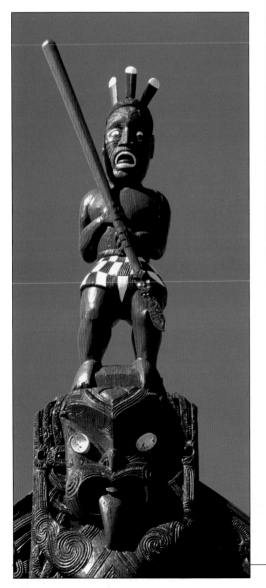

ABORIGINAL CREATION MYTH

Long ago, in the Dreamtime, or Story Time, the ancestral beings came out of a flat, featureless landscape. They had many forms: usually they were animals or birds—kangaroos, crocodiles, snakes, emus, and hawks—but they were also insects, plants, and even hollow logs, clouds, and rain. Sometimes they took human form; often they were giants.

Traveling across the land, hunting and gathering, they made and named all of its features, each of their actions leaving a mark. Where the great ancestral snakes wriggled, rivers were formed; where the ancestral dingo curled up to sleep, a deep bowl was left in the land. The ancestral emu egg became a giant rock, and where an ancestor stuck his spear into the ground, a cabbage palm tree was made.

In Cape York, for example: *The Two Brothers chopped down a giant tree. All the chips flew everywhere and became other trees, all different kinds. Every time a chip flew, they'd name it. That's how all the trees came, and all the plants, grass lilies, and everything, and all the minya [animals]. They would sing out the names as they were chopping.*

When they had made the land, the ancestors "sat down" into it, their resting places becoming sacred sites. Each became a totem for the clan responsible for taking care of that part of the land and its "story places."

An Aboriginal bark painting depicts Dreamtime figures.

Throughout the islands of the Pacific and Indian Oceans, woodcarving is the main mythic art. Carved objects include statues, bowls, war clubs, and the prows of canoes. In New Zealand, the Maori people carve house lintels like this one, showing a god and a warrior.

Aboriginal Stories

The most important mythological being in Aboriginal Australia is the Rainbow Serpent. It can be compared with the Mesopotamian *Tiamat* and the serpent figures of the Orient. In Oceania it is linked with the rainbow and rain: symbols of the world's fertility. For example, Rongo, the Maori god of agriculture (called Lono in Hawaii, or Lo'o in Samoa), appears as a rainbow which, as a pathway from Heaven to Earth, represents humankind's mortality.

In Australia, the Rainbow Serpent indicates the power of the land to generate human beings and all other resources. It is the source of rain and of "spirit children," which are often found in waterholes and wells. In several places it is believed that, by touching a rock painting of the Rainbow Serpent, a person from the local clan can cause rain to fall, and a spirit child to become available to "jump up" and animate the fetus in a pregnant woman's womb.

When people die, they "go back to the rainbow." Aboriginal shamans, to gain their special knowledge, have to "pass through the rainbow," and in many parts of Australia the serpent empowers them with sacred quartz crystals, believed to have come from the heavens. Used traditionally for rainmaking ceremonies, these crystals are part of a ritual interaction with the "source of life" that is the Rainbow.

Light, punishment, and protection

Many Oceanic creation myths describe how light emerged from darkness. In Polynesia it is the god Io who separates night and day. Aboriginal Australians describe the making of light as the task of many ancestral beings.

In Australia, rock art dates back more than 30,000 years. Some, like this scene from Laura, North Queensland, show human and animal figures. Others show the marks people and animals leave in the ground.

Dreamtime stories are a vital part of modern Aboriginal life, giving Australia's "First Peoples" a clear sense of identity and an intense attachment to the land. Many communities still hunt and gather and enact their myths through dance, song, and art, to keep in touch with their "ancestral connections."

Strangers are introduced to the ancestral beings at sacred places through formal "baptisms" with water or smoke. When a member of the community dies, traditional funeral rituals are performed so that, like the ancestral beings, their spirit can be returned to its home in the land.

Many Aboriginal myths relate to hunting, fishing and finding one's way round, using weapons such as spears and boomerangs, recognizing landmarks, and generally living off the land.

As well as explaining how the world was made, myths often provide parables of right and wrong. In many Aboriginal stories, ancestral beings who have affairs with the wrong people, or who cheat and steal, invariably suffer death or injury. Punishment is also meted out to those who come into illegal contact with sacred objects or secret knowledge, or who fail to look after their families or their land. The ancestral landscape—along with its lesser ghosts and devils—protects scared places and upholds Aboriginal law.

MYTHS AND MAPS
Aboriginal mythology describes the landscape and its owners. The totemic stories of each clan are its maps and the rights of that clan to that "country." The myths also give detailed information about how to recognize different species and make use of them. Mythic beings gather and cook food, hunt animals, find water, make boomerangs, and generally demonstrate successful hunter-gatherer lives.

EMU AND BROLGA

Many Aboriginal myths describe how places and species were created, providing bush lore and offering a lively drama of crime and punishment. The story of two bird ancestors, Emu and Brolga, recurs in hundreds of different versions all over Australia. This one is from Cape York:

Emu and Brolga were camped beside a waterhole, where they had been collecting lily roots and mussels, and cooking them in the fire. Both had many chicks, but the Emu was jealous of Brolga's children. Hiding all but two of her own babies, she tricked Brolga into killing most of hers by saying there wasn't enough food for so many.

When Brolga realized she had been deceived, she got a digging stick and hit Emu, breaking her back and giving her the bent-over shape she now has. Emu got her yam stick and hit Brolga

over the head, and the blood left the red topknot that brolgas have today. Then Brolga persuaded Emu to reach into the fire to get the food, burning off her wings so that she couldn't fly any more. 'You don't fly, you just run along the ground!'.

Today, Emu can't fly, but she can still have many chicks, while Brolga can only have two. Brolga cried and cried over her lost babies, and flew north, where she "sat down" and became a large stone in the Coleman River.

Melanesian Myths

Making fire from available material—the traditional way. Oceanic myths retell how a trickster god was responsible for stealing fire and bringing it to the world.

The islands of Melanesia range from the 460,000-square kilometer bulk of Papua New Guinea to tiny islets atop coral reefs.

The earliest arrivals to the islands were hunter-gatherers, and archaeologists have found boat pieces from 33,000 years ago. The region has since produced social groups and economies as varied as the landscape: farmers in the central plateau of Papua New Guinea, hunters in the mountains above them, and on the coasts and islands skilled sailors who made a traditional living from the rich tropical seas, paddling from island to island in a *kula* exchange of armshells and necklaces.

Melanesian mythology is diverse but, like the rest of Oceania, it focuses on totemic ancestors and a sentient landscape. Everyday life takes place alongside a lively spirit world inhabited by ancestral beings and more recent ghosts. In many tales, ancestral beings change shape readily: a wooden stake washed away by the sea becomes a crocodile, and men putting on feathered headdresses become birds.

Mimics and messiahs

Oceanic rituals often imitate the actions of mythic beings, enabling the actors to identify with them and draw upon ancestral powers. Many rituals focus on the fertility of the land and its people.

The Marind people's *mayo* ceremonies, enacting the mythic emergence of the ancestral coconut palm, include sexual orgies that evoke the potency of the ancestral *Dema* and encourage new plants to be productive. Would-be lovers belonging to the Elema people impersonate *Papare*, the Moon, who in mythical times was magnetically attractive to women. By calling themselves by the Moon's secret name, *Marai*, men hope to become equally irresistible to the opposite sex.

Early missionary activities in Melanesia produced some new myths. Some myths featured Messiahs who would end the domination of the colonists, and others encouraged "cargo cults," in which the believers stopped producing food and goods in the belief that a mysterious ship would soon appear, bringing a cargo so wonderful that in future no one need ever work again.

YAMS ARE PEOPLE TOO

Melanesia was home to some of the world's first farmers: there is evidence that tubers were cultivated there over 30,000 years ago. Giant yams, some weighing 14–18 kilograms, are powerful mythological objects as well as traditional symbols of wealth and status. Among the islanders of Dobu, yams are seen as having their own ancestral heritage, and are part of particular human families. These yams "agree" to be cultivated only in the ground belonging to "their" people, with the aid of the family's private spells. Seed yams are encouraged to grow through quiet and secret incantations.

We murmur underneath. The yams hear; they say among themselves, "This is our language, not loud like everyday talk." If you call aloud, the yams say, "How is this—are they fighting among themselves?" But when we charm softly, they listen to our speech attentively. They grow big for our calling on them.

At night they come forth from the Earth and roam about. For this reason, if we approach the garden at night, we tread very quietly. We do not dig the harvest when the Sun is low in the morning. We wait till the sun has mounted, then we know that they are back.

A Papua New Guinea highland warrior in traditional dress, with nose piercing, feathered headdress, and necklaces.

Male Trobriand Island villagers carry yams to their village during the yam harvest. The yam, or sweet potato, is a common staple food throughout Oceania. Among the Maori, yams are symbols of fertility and birth.

Seafarers and Storytellers

Stone statues on Easter Island, which the Polynesians call Mata-ki-te-Rangi, *meaning "eyes toward the heavens."*

TAHITIAN CREATION CHANT
He [Ta'aroa] overturned his shell and raised it up to form the sky . . . and he slipped out of another shell that covered him, which he took for rock and sand. But his anger was not yet appeased, so he took his spine for a mountain range, his ribs for mountain slopes, his vitals for the broad fleeting clouds, his flesh for the fatness of the Earth, his arms and legs for the strength of the Earth, his fingernails and toenails for scales and shells for the fishes, his feathers for trees, shrubs and creepers, to clothe the Earth, his intestines for lobsters, shrimps and eels for the rivers and seas. And the blood of Ta'aroa got heated and drifted away for redness for the sky and the rainbows.

The Polynesians are descended from the brave souls who, between 2,000 and 3,000 years ago, set out from Asia and Melanesia in tiny outrigger canoes to colonize the most distant islands of Oceania, including New Zealand (or Aotearoa), Hawaii, Tonga, and the far-off Easter Island. Arriving with domestic animals, they created sizeable communities that lived from horticulture and fishing. However, they also fought each other over territory. Tribal warriors attacked other tribes, launching raids in great war canoes to steal greenstone, kill their enemies, and so gain *mana* (spiritual strength).

Myths of grandeur and conflict
Polynesian mythology reflects these epic journeys and fierce rivalries. A steep hierarchy of gods is led by Io, the supreme being, who lives in the highest of 12 heavens. Io is assisted by a number of sky gods, earthly gods, and others who populate the Underworld.

The array of deities and sacred ancestors provides divine figureheads for the great and prestigious lineages into which many Polynesian tribes are organized. In New Zealand, which the Maoris call Aotearoa, Maori "name lists" take each tribe back to the original canoe landing of the ancestral 'Great Fleet'.

The mythic world of Polynesia often describes great conflict and division. The major task of the creator god, Ta'aroa ("the severer,") was to separate night and day and Earth and sky, dividing the cosmos into *po*, the world of darkness, the original gods and the dead, and *ao*, the world of light and human life. This Ta'aroa did by dividing up his own body.

STATUES
The statues are 3–12 meters tall and weigh up to 80 tonnes. They are erected on a stone platform and face inland. Each statue consists of a torso and head—the *moai*—and, usually, a topknot, or *pukao*. The eyes are mostly "blind" but there is evidence that the eye cavities were filled with white coral and a central pumice or red-rock iris so that the figures appear to gaze slightly upward.

CREMATION PITS
Between the statue platform and the sea were numerous cremation pits. These may have been used to cremate people or animals.

Traditional canoe

SACRED VESSELS
Maori priests–*tohunga*–being the human receptacles for spiritual knowledge, are sometimes called *waka atua* ("god's canoe.") They conduct ceremonies in strict accordance with ritual law, or *tapu*. Since the 19th century, many of these ceremonies have been carried out in Maori meeting houses, called *whare whakairo*, which represent the bodies of ancestors.

CEREMONIAL DWELLING PLACES

Opposite the statue platform, the islanders built oval-shaped houses known as *hare paenga*. The houses had stone foundations and a framework of curved branches covered with long plant stems and fibers. In front of the houses, the islanders made a large flat area and cleared it of vegetation. This plaza was probably used to hold rituals and ceremonies.

Pathways from the houses to the plaza.

Ceremonial plaza

BURIAL CHAMBERS

Alongside the row of statues were a series of funerary pits. Possibly chiefs and society leaders were buried here. However, there is no evidence of elaborate funeral processions or burial rituals having taken place.

EASTER ISLAND CEREMONIAL PLATFORMS

Easter Island, in the South Pacific Ocean, was first settled around 400 A.D., probably by Polynesians but possibly by South American Indians. The early islanders carved and erected huge stone statues to honor their ancestors. They called them *aringa ora*, or "living faces." More than 600 of these statues are still standing.

Precisely how or why the statues were erected is uncertain, but they are linked with special platforms, burial chambers, and houses where priests and chiefs lived. Whatever rituals, customs, traditions, and myths may have been linked with the giants is a matter of conjecture.

EARTH MOTHERS

Mother Earth is fervently celebrated in Polynesian mythology. In Mangaia (the Cook Islands), Vari, the Great Mother, is seen as central to the fecundity of the islands and to the gods' ability to generate humankind, while in Tikopia women have their own divine patroness and a female cult from which men are firmly excluded.

Powerful female goddesses abound: in Hawaii: Pele, the volcano goddess of Mount Kilauea is said to demand human victims when she is angry. In Maori mythology, Hine-nui-te-po, the goddess of death, devoured the demigod hero Maui, and so created human mortality. Inhabiting the underworld, she is the dark womb to which humankind returns.

DIVINE MAORIS

In Maori mythology, the world came out of a great Nothingness, Te Kore. The Great Night was followed by many ages of Darkness until Te Ata, the Dawn. Out of the dark primeval womb came a divine couple, Rangi, the sky god, and Papa, the Earth Mother. Their passionate cosmic embrace was finally separated by their son Tane-mahuta, the god of forests, birds, and insects.

Tane-mahuta, with his strong limbs planted firmly on mother Earth, was the only one of their six children strong enough to push the sky upwards and make room for human beings.

He persuaded Tu-matauenga, the god of war, not to kill Rangi and Papa, but to join forces with him alongside Tangaroa, god of the ocean, Rongo-matane, the god of peace and of the sweet potato, and Huamia-tike-tike, god of the fern root. They helped Tane to battle against Whiro, who personifies darkness, evil and death and inhabits the Underworld, and Tawhiri-matea, the god of winds and tempests.

Having made a space, Tane also provided a mother for humankind. He created Hine-ahuone from red earth and breathed life into her.

Ancestral Powers

The basis of myths of Oceania—clear skies, clear oceans, and tiny ribbons of land.

THE RISING OF THE SEA
For the people of Vanuatu, the sea itself was made in the primordial epoch, when the creator *Barkulkul* and his two brothers left the sky world and slid to Earth down the trunk of a coconut palm. The myth echoes some of the flood stories from northern Australia:

In the beginning there was no sea, only land. One day, the men of Pan Taiyial were planting their yams. The sun was very hot and they were thirsty. Two women went to collect water in a wild taro leaf. As they returned, the thorns of a liana pierced the leaf, and the water ran onto the ground in a huge expanse. The water kept rising. At first, it was not deep and they told the men they could go in, but the men drowned. The women took wood and threw it into the sea, and the sea became dark and blue.

Maui (known by many names across Oceania) is one of the Maori "heroes" whose great deeds, like those of the Australian ancestors, formed the features of the world. He captured and beat the Sun so that it could only crawl across the sky, and pulled up a giant fish, which became the North Island of Aotearoa. His willingness to die by entering the Underworld is at the heart of the warrior ethos, in which *mana* is gained through bravery and sacrifice.

In Hawaiian mythology, Paka'a, the god of winds and grandson of the creator Loa, invented the sail for Polynesian mariners, and in Fiji, Rokola, the carpenter god, who showed people how to build boats, became identified with Noah when Christian missionaries reached the island.

Micronesian tradition and myth
The tiny islands of Micronesia are dotted with small and scattered settlements. Like the rest of Oceania, many of the islands are hundreds of kilometers from their neighbors. Traditionally dependent on staple foods such as yams, taro, and breadfruit as well as seafoods, the people of each island also produced a "speciality" for exchange with other islands. Some made fine mats or shell ornaments. The Yap islanders used to sail to Palau to quarry for the large stone discs used for "money." Like Polynesian societies, Micronesians have great ancestral lineages, and nobles with special religious responsibilities.

On Ulithi Atoll in the Caroline Islands, Micronesia, ceremonies recalling myths of invaders from the sea are still performed.

Guiding lights

From such minute specks of land it is unsurprising that Micronesian mythology looks skyward, worshiping the Sun, and gods such as Aluluei, whose thousands of eyes are the guiding stars. As in Polynesia, there is a sacred era centered on the separation of Earth and sky.

In Kiribati (the Gilbert Islands), the myth is described thus:

The sky and the Earth clove together, until the creator Naareau sacrificed the first primeval being, and used his eyes to make the Sun and the Moon. This enabled a "Company of Spirit Fools" to haul the First Land from the depths.

Naareau also ensnares the cosmic eel Riiki, and flings him overhead to become the Milky Way, in an echo of the story of the Rainbow Serpent. Divine "worms" also feature in Marshall Island mythology, in which the first man and woman, *Wulleb* and *Lejman*, were worms who lived in a great shell, until they split it into two to make the sky and the Earth.

MYTHOLOGY AND MODERNITY

Oceanic mythology has proved very resilient. Some details have been lost during two centuries of colonization and missionary activity, but often people simply added Christianity as an extra layer, or drew parallels between Biblical stories and their own. In northern Australia, as in Fiji, Noah has been adopted as a "Flood Story" ancestor, and accounts of *Io* in Polynesia have proved quite compatible with Christian beliefs about a "supreme being."

Oceanic mythology remains vital, partly because the ancestral stories define who people are, providing them with a totemic clan or lineage, and a clear sense of identity. By conferring rights to land and resources, mythology has also become a critical part of the land rights movements, for example in Australia and Aotearoa.

Oceanic societies now have economies largely centered on tourism, and their mythology is important here too. The telling of ancestral stories through songs and performance, or in paintings and sculptures, is a useful way of teaching others about indigenous cultures. However, artists painting Dreamtime images or performing island dances are not merely educating tourists, they are also passing their culture on to the next generation, and participating in spiritual life. Some groups are reviving increase ceremonies and initiations.

For many Oceanic peoples, the ancestral forces are still very much present in the land, in sacred objects, and their actions, and more and more they are willing to share this knowledge with strangers and outsiders.

A Maori with facial tatoos and chanting the warlike haka *brings the power of the ancestors into another new millennium.*

Mythology in the Future

In recent times, Buddhism has spread far and wide around the world as increasing numbers of young people have traveled to Buddhist countries. Buddhist thoughts, beliefs, art, and myths are influencing western culture.

As this book hopefully makes clear, mythology is the critical fuel that feeds societies, that binds each generation to those which follow. Each culture, in its own way and fashion, depends on these vital stories not only to pass on the values of the past, but to insure the principles of the future. Mythic stories are, at their very core, explanations of life. They attempt to answer such important questions as, Why do people die?, Why does evil still exist?, Why did our crops fail?

Thus, since myths and mythologies grapple with these eternal questions, and since we humans inexorably seek after meaning, the future of mythology is bright. Not only will peoples still want answers to life's tough questions, but they will need to know that everyday events are not meaningless, and that their lives count for something.

It is in the academe where the future of mythology may be more checkered. Not long ago, myths were relegated into the purview of English departments, the stuff of fiction and fantasy. Worse yet, some scholars were convinced that myths attracted only the "primitive" societies or the mentally suspect, and that with the maturation of cultures, the need for myths would disappear. Happily, such reductionistic thinking has been superseded by more sophisticated and holistic analyses.

The scholarly literature today suggests that there is a growing recognition of the wide spectrum of mythologies, and an accompanying awareness that most speak to the deepest needs of human beings. Thus, while it is certainly true that academia prides itself on keeping a respectful distance from personal involvement in those personal realms so often enriched by mythology, it is nonetheless certain that most scholars are open to acknowledging the rich contributions of mythology. As the resurgence in popular religion suggests, such openness echoes the attitudes of most people living in society, and speaks well to the future of mythology.

Bibliography

Introduction
Eliade, Mircea. *Myth and Reality*. New York: Harper and Row, 1963.
Levi-Strauss, Claude, *From Honey to Ashes. Introduction to the Science of Mythology*. (Multi-volume set). New York: Harper, 1973.
Miller, Dean, *The Epic Hero*. Johns Hopkins University Press, 2000.
Ann, Martha, and Imel, Dorothy Myers, *Goddesses in World Mythology*. Oxford: Oxford University Press, 1995.
Campbell, Joseph, *Historical Atlas of World Mythology* (three volumes). New York: Harper and Row, 1988.
Mercatante, Anthony, *The Facts on File Encyclopedia of World Mythology and Legend*. New York: Facts on File, 1988.
Cotterell, Arthur, *A Dictionary of World Mythology*. Oxford University Press, 1991.
Willis, Roger (ed.), *World Mythology: An Illustrated Guide*. London: Duncan Baird Publishers, 1993.
Alexander, Murray, *Who's Who in Mythology: A Classic Guide to the Ancient World*. Wings Books, 1988.
Morford, Mark (ed.), *Classical Mythology*. Oxford: Oxford University Press, 2000.

Mesopotamia
Coogan, Michael, *Stories from Ancient Canaan*. Philadelphia: Westminster Press: 1978.
Dalley, Stephanie, *Myths from Mesopotamia. Creation, the Flood, Gilgamesh, and others*. Oxford: O.U.P., 1991.
Driver, G.R.,*Canaanite Myths and Legends* (2nd revised ed.) Edinburgh: Clark, 1978.
Gray, John, *Near Eastern Mythology*, London: Hamlyn, 1982.
Hunter, Erica C,D., *First Civilizations: Cultural Atlas for Young People*. Oxford, New York: Facts on File, 1994.
McCall, Henrietta, *Mesopotamian Myths*. London: British Museum Publications, 1990.
Pritchard, James, *Ancient Near Eastern Texts Relating to the Old Testament* (3rd edition) Princeton, N.J., 1969.

Ancient Egypt
Hornung, Erik, *Conceptions of God in Ancient Egypt*. Ithaca: Cornell University Press; London: Routledge, 1982/3.
Meeks, D. and Farvard-Meeks C., *Daily Life of the Egyptian Gods*. London: Pimlico, 1999.
Clark, R. T. R., *Myth and Symbol in Ancient Egypt*. London: Thames and Hudson, 1959.
Shafer, Byron E. (ed.) *Religion in Ancient Egypt*. Ithaca: Cornell University Press; London: Routledge, 1991.
Sattin, A., *The Pharaoh's Shadow*. London: Gollancz, 2000.

Greece
Burkert, Walter, *Greek Religion*. Cambridge, MA: Harvard University Press, 1985.
Gantz, Timothy, *Early Greek Myth Volumes I and II*. Baltimore and London: Johns Hopkins University Press, 1993.
Harris, Stephen L. and Platzner, Gloria, *Classical Mythology: Images and Insights*. 2nd ed. Mountain View, CA: Mayfield Publishing, 1998.
Powell, Barry B., *Classical Myth*. Englewood Cliffs, NJ: Prentice-Hall, 1995.
Vernant, Jean-Pierre, *Myth and Society in Ancient Greece*. Trans. Janet Lloyd. New York: Zone Books, 1990.
Veyne, Paul, *Did the Greeks Believe Their Myths?* Chicago and London: The University of Chicago Press, 1988.

Rome
Adkins, Lesley and Adkins, Roy A., *Dictionary of Roman Religion*. New York: Facts on File, Oxford, New York, 1996.
Bremmer, J.N. and Horsfall, N.M., *Roman Myth and Mythography*. London: University of London,

Institute of Classical Studies, 1987.
Ferguson, John, *The Religions of the Roman Empire*. Ithaca, NY: Cornell University Press, 1970.
Gardner, Jane F., *Roman Myths*. Austin, TX and Great Britain: University of Texas Press and British Museum Press, 1993.
Grant, Michael, *Roman Myths*. New York, Scribner, 1972.
Scullard, H.H., *Festivals and Ceremonies of the Roman Republic*. Ithaca, NY: Cornell University Press, 1981.

Northern Europe
Cotterell, Arthur, *The Encyclopedia of Mythology*. London: Lorenz Books, 1999.
Crossley-Holland, Kevin, *The Penguin Book of Norse Myths*. Harmondsworth: Penguin, 1980.
Davidson, H.R.Ellis, *Gods and Myths of Northern Europe*. Harmondsworth: Penguin, 1964.
Delaney, Frank, *Legends of the Celts*. London, Sydney, Aukland, Toronto: Hodder and Stoughton, 1995.
Mac Cana, Proinsias, *Celtic Mythology*. Chancellor Press, London, Aukland, Melbourne,Singapore, Toronto: Chancellor Press, 1996.
MacKillop, James, *Dictionary of Celtic Mythology*. Oxford, New York: Oxford University Press, 1998.
Orchard, Andy, *Dictionary of Norse Myth and Legend*. London, New York: Cassell, 1997.

Central and Eastern Europe
Cotterell, Arthur (ed.), *World Mythology*, Bath: Dempsey Parr, 1999.
Dixon-Kennedy, Mike, *Encyclopedia of Russian and Slavic Myth and Legend*. California: ABC-CLIO, 1998.
Dixon-Kennedy, Mike, *European Myth and Legend*. London: Blandford, 1997.
Kirby, W.F. (Trans.), *Kalevala*. London: The Athlone Press, 1985.
Simonov, Pyotr, *Essential Russian Mythology*. London: Thorsons, 1997.
Wilkinson, Philip, *Illustrated Dictionary of Mythology*. London: Dorling Kindersley, 1998.
Willis, Roy (ed.), *World Mythology*. London: Piatkus, 1997.

Africa
Geoffrey Parrinder, *African Mythology*. London: Chancellor Press, 1996.
Jan Knappert, *Kings, Gods and Spirits from African Mythology*. London: Peter Lowe, 1986.
Jan Knappert, *African Mythology*. London: Aquarian, 1990.
Ngangar Mbitu and Ranchor Prime, *Essential African Mythology*. London: Thorsons, 1997.
Jan Knappert, *Myths and Legends of the Congo*. Nairobi: Heinemann Educational, 1971.

India
A. C. Bhaktivedanta Swami, *Srimad Bhagavatam*, Los Angeles: Bhaktivedanta Book Trust, 1975.
Ranchor Prime, *Ramayana: A Journey*. London: Collins and Brown, 1997.
Wendy O'Flaherty, *Hindu Myths*. London: Penguin Books, 1975.
Wendy O'Flaherty, *The Rig Veda*. London: Penguin Books, 1981.
A.L.Basham, *The Sacred Cow*. London: Rider, 1989.
J.M. Macfie, *Myths and Legends of India*. Republished in Calcutta, Rupa & Co., 1993.

China and South-east Asia
Joanne O'Brien, *Elements of Feng Shui*. Shaftesbury: Element, 1991.
Martin Palmer and Jay Ramsay, *Tao Te Ching, Chapter 1*, translated by Man-Ho Kwok. Shaftesbury: Element, 1993.
Martin Palmer, *Travels Through Sacred China*. London: Thorsons, 1996.
Martin Palmer, *Elements of Taoism*. Shaftesbury: Element, 1991.
Zhao Xiamin, *Essential Chinese Mythology*. London: Thorsons, 1997.

Martin Palmer, Jay Ramsay, Zhao Xiaomin, *I Ching*, trans. London: Thorsons, 1995.
Martin Palmer, Jay Ramsay and Kwok Man-Ho, *Kuan Yin*. London: Thorsons, 1995.
Kwok Man-Ho, *The Eight Immortals*. London: Rider, 1990.

North America
Erdoes, Richard, and Ortiz, Alfonso, eds., *American Indian Myths and Legends*. New York: Random House, 1984.
Kane, Sean, *Wisdom of the Mythtellers*. Peterborough (Ontario, CA):Broadview Press, 1994.
Larson, Robert, *Red Cloud: Warrior-Statesman of the Lakota Sioux*. Norman: University of Oklahoma Press, 1997.
Ramsey, Jarold, ed., *Coyote was Going There* (Indian Literature of the Oregon Country). Seattle: University of Washington Press, 1977.
Ruby, Robert, and Brown, John A. *Dreamer-Prophets of the Columbia Plateau*. Norman: University of Oklahoma Press, 1989.
Splawn, A.J., Kamiakin, *The Last Hero of the Yakamas*.Caldwell:Caxton Printers, 1980 ed.
Strong, Emory, *Stone Age on the Columbia River*. Portland: Binford and Mort, 1959.
Velie, Alan R., *American Indian Literature: An Anthology*. Norman: University of Oklahoma Press, 1991.

Central and South America
Betanzos, Juan de, *Narrative of the Incas*, translated by Roland Hamilton; Austin: Texas University Press, 1996
Cobo, Bernabi, *Inca Religion and Customs*, translated by Roland Hamilton; Austin: Texas University Press, 1990.
Mosely, Michael E, *The Incas and their Ancestors: The archaeology of Peru*. London: Thames and Hudson, 1992.
Rostworowski de Diez Canseco, Maria, *History of the Inca Realm*, translated by Harry B. Iceland. Cambridge University Press, 1999.
Coe, Michael D., *The Maya*. London: Thames and Hudson, 1987.
Tedlock, Dennis (translator and editor), *Popol Vuh: The Mayan book of the dawn of life*. New York: Touchstone Books, 1985.
Lizot, Jacques *Tales of the Yanomami: Daily life in the Venezuelan Forest*. Cambridge University Press, 1985.
Riviore, Peter, *Marriage among the Trio*. Oxford: Oxford University Press, 1985.

Oceania
Coppet, D. and Iteanu, A. (eds), *Cosmos and Society in Oceania*, Oxford: Berg, 1995.
Eliade, M., *Australian Religions: an introduction*. Ithaca and London: Cornell University Press, 1973.
Hiatt, L.R. (ed), *Australian Aboriginal Mythology*. Canberra: Australian Institute of Aboriginal Studies, 1975.
Knappert, J., *Pacific Mythology: an encyclopedia of myth and legend*. London: The Aquarian Press, 1992.
Lewis, D. and Forman, W., *The Maori: heirs of Tane*. London: Orbis, 1982.
MacKenzie, M., *Androgynous Objects: string bags and gender in central New Guinea*. Chur, Reading, Paris, Philadelphia, Tokyo, Melbourne: Harwood Academic Publishers, 1991.
Malinowski, B., *Argonauts of the Western Pacific: an account of native enterprise and adventure in the archipelagoes of Melanesian New Guinea*. London: Routledge and Kegan Paul, 1922.
Rose, D., Dingo *Makes Us Human: life and land in an Aboriginal Australian culture*. Cambridge: Cambridge University Press, 1992.
Strang, V., *Uncommon Ground: cultural landscapes and environmental values*. Oxford, New York: Berg, 1997.
Swain, T. and Trompf, G., *The Religions of Oceania*. London, New York: Routledge, 1995.

Glossary of Mythological Terms

Absinth European herb, often called "the accursed herb," also known as "wormwood," often mentioned in the Hebrew and Christian scriptures.

A.D. Anno Domini, Latin for "in the year of our Lord," a way of counting years following the birth of Christ. C.E., "Common Era," is often used as an alternative.

Aesir The Norse gods of war, death, and power, who reside in Asgard.

Afterlife A world peopled by spirit creatures, which functions as a "parallel universe" to our present world; a pervasive belief found in numerous mythologies.

Akkad The northern portion of Mesopotamia, now modern Iraq, and the name of the capital city built by Sargon, founder of the Akkadian Dynasty.

Amazonia Tropical lowland region of South America, inhabited by small, tribal societies.

Amulet *See* Talisman.

Animism The belief that all of nature (including rocks, mountains, and geographic regions) may be alive, and may also possess or harbor spirits.

Anthropomorphism The attribution of human characteristics or emotions to animals or things.

Aryan A Sanskrit term describing human civilization based on spiritual principles often used to depict the ancient religion and civilization that were ancestors to both the Indian and Iranian civilizations, flourishing approximately 2000 B.C.

Asgard One of the worlds of the Norse universe, and home to many of the Norse deities (*see* Aesir).

Ashanti Tribe occupying part of modern Ghana, who were among the first trading partners with the European powers in the colonial period.

Atman/Atma A term that originally meant "breath," but came to signify the immortal self or soul in Indian religion.

Bank of Hell In Chinese mythology, currency notes from the "Bank of Hell" are burned in order to make hell more bearable, and to bribe officials in the afterlife.

B.C. Before Christ, a way of counting years before the birth of Jesus Christ. B.C.E., "Before the Common Era" is often used as an alternative. *See also* A.D.

Bush lore Especially in Australian myth, referring to intimate knowledge about the environment.

Bush name In Australia, a personal name referring to an ancestral totem or part of ancestral myth.

Coricancha Inca temple and center for religious worship in Cuzco, famous for its garden of gold and silver plants and trees.

Corroborree The performance of an ancestral story through song, dance, or theater (Australia).

Cosmic renewal In Chinese mythology, this refers to the continuing supplication of the Taoist priests to maintain the delicate balance of Yin and Yang. If the balance is not maintained, chaos will result.

Cosmogony A myth that usually deals specifically with the creation and/or maintenance of the universe.

Cosmos Literally, "order, universe," usually referring to the moral and divine structure of the universe.

Craft In Native American societies, the highly prized ability to use one's wits to outsmart a foe who might be physically stronger.

Cuneiform The ancient, wedge-shaped script of Akkadian, which was written on clay tablets and used throughout Mesopotamia and Israel.

Deva A Sanskrit term for the deity, or specifically, for the deities that embody an aspect of nature, such as Agni, the god of fire, Vayu, the god of wind, or Ganga, the goddess of the River Ganges in India.

Divination In various religious mythologies, practices (such as consulting departed ancestors or observing natural phenomena) thought to predict misfortunes and offer advice on how to avoid them.

Djed-Pillar In Egyptian religion, an amulet modeled after Osiris, and often associated with mummies.

Dreamers/Dreamer Prophets in North American mythology; people who had died (and hence had been "dreaming"), visited their ancestors, and return to give their tribes the benefit of the ancestors' wisdom.

Druids Priests and counselors who held exceptional power in Celtic society; also refers to religious groups in general that venerate and worship objects of nature. *See* Eco-religions.

Dwarfs In Norse mythology, wise craftsmen who dwelt among the rocks, and out of the light of day.

Earth Goddess In some early agricultural societies, the deity that represented the Earth and was thought responsible for a successful harvest.

Eco-religions (or Nature religions) Religions whose practices are perceived to be more in harmony with the environment than are traditional religions.

Elder In Native American peoples, an esteemed, usually older, tribal member, who holds positions of leadership, and is often responsible for passing on oral tradition.

Epagomenal days Celebrated in Egypt as the birthdays of the gods, these days were added to each year to insure the correctness of the calendar.

Etiology From the Greek *aitios*, meaning "cause," etiological stories provide explanations and sources of names, rituals, and customs.

Evil Spirits In many mythological traditions, spirit beings that can take on human or animal forms at will, and can be a source of fear to worshipers.

Feng Shui Literally "wind and water," this refers to an assumption that humans should strive to be a harmonious part of a living universe, and that building designs ought to conform to the dynamics of mountain, hill, river, and the shape of the land.

Furies In Greek mythology, these female creatures pursued children who committed patricide or matricide.

Gorgons Three divine sisters who had living snakes for hair and could turn men into stone with their gaze. One of the Gorgons, Medusa, was mortal and was slain by the hero Perseus.

Grail Sometimes called the "Holy Grail," believed to be the chalice from which Jesus drank at the Last Supper. Stories and myths arose across Northern Europe about King Arthur and his knights and their "quests" to find and possess the Grail.

Guru Literally, "one who is heavy with knowledge," a spiritual teacher or guide who passes on wisdom to followers seeking knowledge.

Huaca Inca shrine, holy place, or object of veneration.

Hungry Ghosts Ghosts with nobody to look out for them who are thought to wander the afterlife in a constant state of anxiety. Such ghosts are often thought to torment the living.

Hunter-gatherer society A mobile culture that subsists by hunting game and gathering roots, berries, and other wild foods, often following the wild game as it migrates. *See* Nomads.

Icon Image usually associated with Greek or Russian Orthodox Christianity, portraying Jesus, the Virgin Mary, or the Saints.

Idol An object of worship, usually a physical depiction of a god.

Illuminated manuscript Beautifully decorated manuscript and handwritten book, produced in Europe between the 5th and late 15th centuries A.D.

Immortality Eternal life: in many traditions immortality is viewed as the ultimate goal of this life.

Imram Irish tales of voyages to the Otherworld.

Inca Huge Andean civilization in South America that once stretched from southern Colombia to northern Argentina. The title "Inca" was used for the ruler of the Inca empire, which was conquered by Pizarro.

Incantation Spell designed to protect people from evil spirits, especially those spells recited by priests attached to Mesopotamian temples.

Internalization Taking a myth to heart, living according to the values and principles taught in the myth.

Inti For the Incas, the name for the Sun, and the male divine ancestor.

Ka In Egyptian religion, an idea that is similar to the western concept of "soul."

Kantele In Finno-Ugric mythology, a five-stringed instrument made by Vainamoinen from the jawbone of a huge pike.

Khipu Inca device for recording information by means of knotted cords.

Kula/Kula ring A traditional system of exchange between a "ring" of islands in the Trobriands.

Language group A group defined by a specific language; may include a number of different clans.

Law (Aboriginal) The "Law" is used to describe a whole body of traditional Aboriginal knowledge, including the ancestral stories.

Maenad A female worshiper of Dionysus who participated in rituals honoring the god of wine. Maenads were also called "Bacchae" or "Bacchants."

Magic Forms of ritualized and non-ritualized behaviors thought to portray the influence of the spirit world upon the physical realm (for example, that physical illnesses have spiritual causes).

Majority culture Term describing non-indigenous culture (especially in North America).

Materialism In philosophy, the school of thought that denies the reality of a spiritual or non-material realm.

Maya Mesoamerican civilization in southern Mexico and Guatemala which constructed the temples of Tikal and Palenque.

Mead An intoxicating drink; in Norse mythology, the "Mead of Poetry" gave drinkers the powers of verse and scholarship.

Medicine man (also Witchdoctor or Shaman) Known by different names; in Africa called Nganga and Babalawo; a person thought to have special powers and abilities in communicating with the spirit world; similar to the shaman of both Siberia and North America.

Mesopotamia Literally meaning "between the rivers," the region of the Rivers Tigris and Euphrates, now in Iraq. The northern region was called Akkad, the southern lands Sumer.

Metamorphoses Greek word meaning "transformation;" the name of a poetic work by the Roman author Ovid, written at the end of the 1st century A.D.

Metis Wife of Zeus whose name meant "cunning intelligence," she was swallowed by Zeus to produce Athena.

Midgard In Norse mythology, "Middle Earth," one of nine worlds and the home of human beings.

Millennium One thousand years, can be interpreted either literally or figuratively, and usually describes a period of divine rule.

Minoan From King Minos of Crete, this term applies to the civilizations of prehistoric Crete.

Modernity In philosophy, the age or school of thought that was optimistic about the use of reason (*see* Rationalism), and the possibility of speaking from a neutral standpoint.

Mukti/Moksha In Hinduism, liberation from the cycle of birth and rebirth (*see* Samsara), somewhat equivalent to the western concept of "salvation" in its release from personal effort and strife.

Mycenaean Term used to describe the art, architecture and culture of Greece from 1600–1200 B.C.

Myth A story or narrative that explains the values and important elements of a society.

Native Americans Those peoples who migrated to the Americas between 7,000 and 35,000 years ago, sometimes called "Indians" in various contexts.

Niflheim The dark world in Norse cosmology, home of the infernal goddess Hel.

Nomads Wandering peoples who subsist by shepherding flocks or by hunting wild game. *See* Hunter-gatherer society.

Norsemen Literally "North Men;" the Indo-European settlers of Northern Europe, particularly Germany and Scandinavia.

Nubia The area south of Egypt, which is now the Sudan.

Nymph A semi-divine creature inhabiting the woods, seas or mountains.

Oracle A shrine offering humans direct access to the wisdom of the Greek gods via a human priest or priestess; also the priest or priestess.

Oral Tradition Through storytelling in either formal or informal settings, the passing down of cultural or tribal values from one generation to another.

Pantheon From the Greek words for "all" and "god," this term refers to all the divinities in a religious system.

Pohjola The northern European regions associated with Lapland.

Polytheism The belief in the existence of many gods and/or goddesses.

Popol Vuh Council Book of the Quiché Maya, which gave an account of their mythology and was also used for divination.

Postmodernism The belief that, in whatever discipline, one inescapably speaks from a point of view, and that true objectivity is impossible.

Primordial Existing from the beginning, first-formed, original.

Rainmaking An important magical function in many desert cultures, especially in Africa, where many practitioners (rainmakers) specialize in this art at various festivals and rituals.

Rationalism In philosophy, the belief in the supremacy of reason in evaluating truth claims. *See also* Materialism and Modernity.

Rituals Formal ceremonies, usually of a recognizably religious nature and performed on a regular basis.

Samsara The Hindu cycle of birth and rebirth, through which each soul must pass, and which only can be broken by salvation. *See* Mukti.

Semitic The family of languages that were widely spoken in Mesopotamia and the Middle East, including Hebrew, Aramaic, and Arabic.

Shaivism The branch of Hinduism that worships Shiva as the supreme deity.

Shaman/Shamaniam Priest or person knowledgeable in the sacred rites of the tribe's myths and spiritual traditions who may be linked with the healing of physical diseases, with the shaman possessing abilities to contact and utilize the powers of the spirit and animal world to influence human society.

Shinto The traditional national religion of Japan, based on the worship of *kami*, indigenous folk deities that fit almost every natural phenomenon. Shinto has no founder, dogma, or sacred scriptures (in the western sense), but venerates the *kami* especially at local Shinto shrines.

Sidhe Irish burial mounds thought by the Celts to be the home of spirits and an entrance to the Otherworld.

Sky God Traditional African mythology usually included a "High God" who was often a Sky God associated with thunder and lightning, and often regarded as a bountiful father to humanity.

Spirit vision quest A rite of passage, usually confined to males at puberty, marked by the participant's isolation, lack of food, and communication with the animal and/or spirit world in order to receive an empowering vision.

Steppe A broad plain, treeless and uncultivated, often with a severe climate, especially in southeast Europe and Asia.

Sumer The southern portion of Mesopotamia, named after the Sumerian peoples who lived there around 4000 B.C.

Sumerian The culture and language of the peoples of Sumer; the language was distinct from the Semitic language group. *See also* Semitic.

Syncretism The adoption or adaptation by a religion, whether intended or not, of another religion's belief(s) and/ or god(s) within its own system of beliefs, often creating an entirely distinct myth.

Tabu/Tapu/Taboo Originally a Polynesian word for things or actions that are forbidden, sacred or otherwise powerful or dangerous. In northern Australia, a similar concept is used to define geography, calling it a "poison place."

Talisman/Amulet A physical object or charm dispensed by the spiritual leader of a group or tribe (*see* Shaman or Medicine man) used to protect people from evil influences, or to procure divine blessing for the wearer.

Tao The traditional religion of China, literally "the Way which cannot be spoken." It exists in many forms, all of which strive to cultivate wisdom and to achieve inner and outer harmony.

Theodicy Literally, "justifying God," meaning the defending of God's existence in a morally ambivalent, or evil world.

Theogony A poem by the Greek poet Hesiod in the 8th–7th century B.C., describing the origins of the universe.

Tirtha Literally, "a place of pilgrimage." The four great Tirthas of India are located at the four corners of the Indian subcontinent.

Torc A Celtic neck ring worn by the gods and people of high rank.

Totem A being (usually animal) that is associated with a certain family or clan, and is thought to provide its sponsors with powers connected with the being; for instance, the hunting prowess of an eagle.

Tribe A group sharing a significant degree of cultural, linguistic, and religious traditions; used increasingly to describe collections of smaller language groups in Oceania.

Trigram The pattern of long and short lines forming the basis of the 64 characters of the *I Ching*, used in divination in Chinese mythology.

Tumulus A burial mound.

Vaishnavism The branch of Hinduism that worships Vishnu as the supreme deity.

Vanir Norse fertility gods who fought against the Aesir. When further fighting was deemed pointless, the two groups of gods exchanged hostages and agreed to coexist peacefully.

Vedas Sanskrit hymns which, in their present form, date back to at least 1500 B.C., and give their name to the Vedic culture of India.

Viking Warriors and explorers from Scandinavia who raided Europe between the 8th and 11th centuries A.D.

Viracocha Supreme deity and creator of Inca pantheon of gods.

Votive offering A prized possession sacrificed to the gods as a sign of good faith or to enlist their help.

Washani/Washaat A Native American religion begun in the 19th century by Smohalla, a Dreamer Prophet of the Pacific northwest part of what is now the United States. Its key element was its rejection of agriculture and other European-American practices.

Yin/Yang The passive and active principles, respectively, that Chinese religion and philosophy identify as comprising the struggle inherent in all of life. Yang is hot, earthy, and male; Yin is cool, watery, and female. Some mythologies portray these principles as the "essences of Heaven and Earth."

Yoga Literally "union with the Supreme" exercises for the body and mind. The four principal forms of Yoga are Karmayoga (the path of action), Jnanayoga (the path of knowledge), Bhaktiyoga (the path of devotion) and Hathayoga (the path of physical and mental exercises leading to the total absorption in God).

Yoruba Tribe occupying part of modern Nigeria who believe in the divine creation of their culture, which is held to be the origin of all other tribes and languages.

Ziggurat A huge temple or tower made of stone and brick, usually with a shrine on the top, round which stairs were constructed for access, found throughout Mesopotamia.

Index